The Book On

Strategic Obsession

How to Turn Long-Term Thinking
Into a Competitive Weapon

The Book On Series

David Webb

Published by The Book On Publishing, 2025.

First edition. July 23, 2025.

I0458767

Website: https://thebookon.ca
Substack: https://thebookonpublishing.substack.com/

The Book On Strategic Obsession: How to Turn Long-Term Thinking Into a Competitive Weapon

First edition. July 23, 2025.

Copyright © 2025 The Book On Publishing

ISBN: 978-1-997795-74-2

Written by David Webb

The Book On Series

Table of Contents

Read This First

This is not a book designed to entertain you. It's not here to charm, to soothe, or to hold your hand. It won't dazzle you with stories, metaphors, or motivational fluff. What you're having is a tool, an instruction manual written for people who are serious about learning, executing, and thinking at a higher level.

Every book in The Book On Series is built on a single premise: clarity beats complexity. We believe that when you strip away the noise, the emotions, the marketing spin, and the cultural rituals of "self-help," what's left is raw, unembellished instruction. That's what these books offer.

They are dry by design. Not because we don't care about language or narrative, but because when you're building something that matters, you don't need more distractions. You need a clear architecture. Mental scaffolding. Direction that respects your intelligence.

Each title in this series takes on a specific domain: decision-making, clarity, strategy, leverage, and uncertainty, and drills deep. Not in sweeping generalizations, but in applied frameworks. These are books for builders, operators, founders, tacticians, and thinkers—people who don't just consume knowledge but operationalize it.

You'll find no chapter-long anecdotes here. No self-congratulatory memoirs. No bullet-point platitudes. Instead, what you'll get is structured insight: argument, example, application. The tone is direct. The prose is sober. The ideas are designed to be lifted out and used.

You won't be coddled, but you won't be misled either.

There's a place in the world for lyrical, emotional, story-driven books, and this isn't that place. This is a workspace. A blueprint. A conversation for people who are ready to act, not just absorb.

We respect your time and your intellect.

Welcome to The Book On Series.

Dedication

For the ones who stay obsessed long-term

after the applause fades.

To the builders who work in silence, the thinkers who play the long game, and the leaders who choose clarity over comfort.

You don't just change outcomes, you change culture.

- David Webb

Prologue

The Most Dangerous Idea in the World

The most dangerous idea in the world isn't radical. It isn't loud. It doesn't trend. It rarely gets talked about at all. That's because it hides in plain sight, often mistaken for madness or stubbornness, until it reshapes an entire field, or outlasts everyone else. That idea is an obsession. Not emotional obsession, not chaos disguised as creativity, not addiction to work. But strategic obsession is a focused, intentional, and disciplined commitment to a single idea over years, even decades.

Most people aren't taught to think this way. We live in a culture that celebrates options, pivots, and the appearance of speed. We're told that being well-rounded, flexible, and reactive is the safest way to navigate a changing world. The assumption is that obsession is dangerous, rigid, and unsustainable. And sometimes it is. But the opposite is just as destructive: drifting from one idea to the next, never giving anything enough time to grow deep roots.

You've probably heard the phrase "don't put all your eggs in one basket." It sounds reasonable. But the people who leave an indelible mark on the world almost always ignore it. They don't spread their energy thin across a dozen small pursuits. They double down on one thing. They *become* the basket.

I wrote this book because I've seen both sides of that equation. I've watched people leap from trend to trend, building shallow wins and quick exits that look impressive until the foundation gives out. I've also seen what happens when someone quietly, methodically commits to an idea they believe in, long after the applause stops, long after the market turns its head, long after logic says to give up.

This book is about *that person*.

Strategic obsession isn't about being stubborn. It's not about martyrdom or grinding your soul down to prove a point. It's about direction. In a world of infinite noise and choices, the most incredible luxury is knowing exactly where you're going and being willing to take the long way to get there.

Obsession becomes strategic when it's guided by clarity, measured by systems, and protected by patience. It becomes a weapon when others can't follow you into year nine, or version seventeen, or prototype thirty-six. Because they weren't obsessed, they were merely interested.

The problem is, we don't reward that thinking early on. Obsession is misunderstood. It looks inefficient. It doesn't scale quickly. It's often mistaken for arrogance, self-delusion, or naivety. But later, *much* later, it's called genius. Visionary. Revolutionary. This book is here to bridge that gap. To give language, structure, and support to the kind of thinker who's always felt slightly out of sync with short-term logic.

Each chapter will walk you through the mental models, methods, endurance tactics, and legacy mechanics that separate obsession from burnout, and strategy from fixation. You'll learn how to build systems that make obsession sustainable. How to tell the difference between when to quit and when to double down. And how to create a life, personally or professionally, where the long game is not just viable, but unbeatable.

This is not a book for the easily impressed. It's for the ones who already have a vision, but no map. It's for the ones who've stayed quiet about how big their idea is, because they know it'll take ten years to make it real. It's for people who don't need to win quickly; they need to win the right way.

And if that's you, then this book is not just permission. It's ammunition.

Let's begin.

But before we do, let me offer one warning.

This book will demand that you make peace with being misunderstood for years, possibly decades. Obsession, especially in its early form, will not earn you applause. It may look like failure. It may even *feel* like failure. That's because we've trained ourselves to expect results on a timeline that suits the observer, not the builder. But your obsession doesn't owe the world visibility. It owes you integrity. That's the difference between a trending project and a strategic one: the former performs for others. The latter performs in silence.

There will be moments when your conviction looks delusional, when people you respect question your sanity, your strategy, or your sense of timing. You will want to compromise, not because your vision has changed, but because the weight of patience is heavier than you thought. You'll look around and see others pivoting to success while you're still refining your first premise. You'll be tempted to believe you're behind. You're not. You're just deep. And depth takes time.

Obsession is lonely until it isn't. Then, suddenly, it's obvious.

History is filled with examples of this: people who toiled for decades in obscurity only to be "discovered" once the world finally caught up. What changed? Not their idea. Not their skill. Not even their execution. What changed was perception, and perception always lags reality. Strategic obsession means you operate on *your* timeline, not theirs. And when the world does catch up, you'll be the only one who's not surprised.

This book exists so you don't feel insane during that gap.

It exists so that your obsession can be refined into a structure, not burned out into regret. It's a handbook for the long-term builder, the person who doesn't just want to win but wants to win in a way that no one else can replicate. That kind of victory isn't loud, but it is permanent.

So, if you're still with me, if a part of you has always known that the work you're doing is bigger than the moment you're in, then you're in the right place.

Turn the page.

You already know what needs to be built.

Let's make it unbreakable.

Chapter 1: The Lie of Optionality

Optionality is the darling of modern thinking. You hear it in venture capital circles, on self-improvement podcasts, even in dating advice. Keep your options open. Stay flexible. Don't commit too soon. The idea sounds empowering, like you're refusing to be boxed in, like you're keeping your freedom intact. But there's a darker side to this logic. A side that undermines mastery, erodes momentum, and rewards indecision disguised as intelligence.

The lie of optionality is that more choices equal more power. In truth, more choices often mean more noise. More uncertainty. More delay. The obsession-averse world we live in teaches us that narrowing down is risky, that by going all-in on one thing, you're cutting yourself off from all the others. But obsession flips that logic on its head. It says: cut off all the others *on purpose because* you can't go deep if you're still scanning the surface for something shinier.

Optionality is attractive to the uncommitted. It's a safe place to hide when you're afraid of being wrong. But strategic obsession is not scared of being bad; it's fearful of being shallow. And that fear is precisely what gives it its edge.

We live in an age of infinite access. There are more podcasts, frameworks, playbooks, mentors, and tools available to a 19-year-old on a budget than were available to most Fortune 500 CEOs just thirty years ago. And yet we're paralyzed. Because with all those choices comes a loss of clarity. We become addicted to planning, to research, to "figuring it out" indefinitely. The one thing we never do is *choose*.

The real reason people avoid obsession is that it forces a choice. It demands a bet. It insists that you take a stand, declare a direction, and live with the consequences. That kind of commitment is rare in the modern attention economy. But it's the only path that compounds.

A person pursuing optionality will take a thousand small steps in a hundred different directions. A person possessed by strategic obsession will take a thousand steps forward in one. From the outside, the difference may not be evident at first. But wait five years, then look again. One will have results. The other will have regrets.

There's something quietly tragic about someone who spends their life researching possibilities but never chooses one. They may sound intelligent, even enlightened. But intelligence without execution is just potential. Potential is only powerful when it's pointed somewhere.

This doesn't mean every obsession is worth keeping. But you'll never find the ones that are unless you're willing to let go of the rest. Focus is expensive because it costs you every other version of yourself you could have been. That's the price of depth. That's the cost of meaning.

The obsessional doesn't ask, "What if this doesn't work?" They ask, "What if this *is* the work?" They don't treat their chosen pursuit as a stepping stone. It's not a sandbox or a placeholder. It's a destination. And if it evolves or expands later, that's fine. But the commitment to pursue it deeply is what gives it the power to grow.

Strategic obsession forces a confrontation with yourself. It asks: Do you want to keep chasing the illusion of endless freedom, or are you ready to give up 99 things so you can master one? Most people never make that trade. That's why most people never build anything that lasts.

Optionality makes you feel smart. Obsession makes you smart. Because once you've closed the doors, the only way out is through. You're forced to think harder, dig deeper, and stretch farther than you would if escape were still on the table. Constraints sharpen creativity. Commitment fuels ingenuity. And the longer you stay in the arena, the more the arena starts to bend to your will.

Obsession doesn't guarantee success. But it gives you the only shot at success that matters: the one where your full energy, mind, and time are aligned behind a single aim. Optionality scatters your force. Obsession concentrates it. And in the long run, the concentrated mind wins.

Optionality is how we avoid embarrassment. It's a hedge against public failure, a way to soften the blow of commitment by saying, "I never really meant it." But obsession removes that. You don't get to pretend you weren't serious. You don't get to blame the environment, the algorithm, or the market conditions. Strategic obsession puts your name on the line, your time, your reputation, your legacy. And that's precisely why it works. You either make it work, or you live in full view of why it didn't. That's pressure. And pressure, for those who learn to bear it, breeds clarity.

We're not short on talent. We're short on people who are willing to endure the discomfort of making a choice. Optionality may seem like a luxury. But for those who want to build something lasting, it's a liability. Because while you're busy deciding, someone else is busy becoming.

Obsession isn't a personality flaw. It's a competitive advantage. And the sooner you let go of the lie that more options equal more freedom, the sooner you'll find the one path that matters.

Chapter 2: Attention Is a Scarce Resource

Your most limited resource isn't time. It's attention.

Time moves with or without your consent. But attention is a decision. It's the choice to give a piece of your consciousness to something, and that choice shapes everything. Attention is what makes time valuable. It's the difference between a productive hour and a wasted one, between years of shallow movement and a decade of deep progress. Strategic obsession begins and ends with this truth: the people who guard their attention with discipline build things that outlast them. Everyone else becomes part of someone else's plan.

In the age of the attention economy, your mind is under siege. Your thoughts, your focus, and your ability to concentrate for longer than a headline are now valuable assets. And if you don't defend them, someone else will deploy them. Clicks, alerts, timelines, and metrics are not neutral. They're engineered to fragment you, to split your attention across dozens of shallow inputs. Obsession, by contrast, is a commitment to depth. And depth cannot survive distraction.

You can't fake obsession in a noisy brain. Strategic depth requires cognitive silence, not just once a week during a digital detox, but as a regular condition of your life. That doesn't mean you need to live in a cave. It means you need to construct your environment so that attention becomes a natural byproduct of how you move through the world. And that starts with a radical revaluation of what you let into your mental ecosystem.

When you're pursuing something meaningful over the years, attention becomes a form of capital. It's not infinite. It compounds when focused, but dissolves when spread thin. If your obsession is the business, attention is the funding. You wouldn't give a stranger access to your bank account. Why give them unfettered access to your head?

People love to say they're multitasking. That they can balance calls, timelines, Slack, email, and still find time to write their novel or build their prototype. But that's a fantasy. Every cognitive switch costs something. Research calls it "attention residue", the mental drag you carry from one task into the next. Obsession doesn't tolerate residue. It requires full mental presence. And full presence can't be achieved while toggling between dopamine hits.

The most productive people in history, the most visionary thinkers, were not necessarily more talented. But they were better at staying with a thought. That's all. They knew how to sit with a problem without escape. To wrestle with complexity instead of running to novelty. They protected their attention like it was a sacred site, and it was.

You don't need monk-like isolation to build something great. But you do need boundaries. Strategic obsession forces you to become unavailable to anything that isn't aligned. That might look like refusing meetings without a clear agenda. It might mean scheduling thinking time with the same gravity you'd assign to investor calls or deadlines. It might mean logging out, turning off, disappearing for a while. Not to retreat, but to go deeper.

The enemy of obsession is scattered effort. Not because you're lazy, but because you're overstimulated. A mind exposed to too much input can't hear its signal. And that signal, the deep thread of your work, is what guides your long game. Lose the signal, and everything becomes reactive. You start chasing trends, mimicking others, breaking your stride to respond to noise. That's how obsession turns brittle. That's how direction gets lost.

Guarding your attention isn't about purity. It's about control. It's about building a mental operating system where your deepest work has room to breathe, where you don't constantly feel behind, distracted, or fractured, where you're not making decisions from a place of noise, but from a place of internal coherence.

Attention isn't just a resource. It's a diagnostic tool. Where it flows, your priorities follow. If your calendar is full of things that don't align with your obsession, that's not a scheduling issue. That's a strategic one. It means your mission hasn't become non-negotiable yet. When it does, the world doesn't shrink; it sharpens.

You'll be called antisocial. You'll be told you're missing out. And maybe you are, on things that don't matter. But you're not here to sample everything. You're here to build something *specific*. And specificity requires saying no, not once, but constantly.

The longer you can stay with a single problem, a single system, a single vision, the more leverage you accumulate. Others will exhaust themselves chasing novelty. You'll compound your insight. Not because you're smarter. But because your mind was available long enough to learn something, they never stuck around to see.

When you protect your attention, you do more than defend your focus. You defend your future. You create a sanctuary where the obsession can evolve, uninterrupted by triviality. You learn how to think again. How to go deep again. How to be alone with a question until the answer finally surfaces.

In a distracted world, attention is rebellion. And the rebel, not the conformist, is the one who changes the game.

Chapter 3: The Death of Novelty

Novelty is addictive.

It triggers the brain's reward system in the same way gambling does, fast, unpredictable, and shallow. You scroll for novelty, shop for novelty, date for novelty, and even read for novelty. And for a few minutes, it works. Your mind lights up. Everything feels new, possible, exciting. But novelty, like sugar, burns fast. It offers stimulation, not nourishment. And in the long run, it leaves you empty.

The culture has sold us the myth that new is always better. That progress is the product of constant change, and that freshness guarantees relevance. In this climate, repetition is treated like death, and mastery is mistaken for stagnation. But obsession tells a different story. Obsession doesn't crave novelty; it destroys it. Because once you've truly committed to an idea, a mission, a long arc of purpose, what matters is not how new something is, but how deep it can go.

Depth is boring at first. It's uncomfortable. It looks like doing the same thing again. It feels like standing still while the world passes by. But underneath that stillness is motion. Compounding. Refinement. A kind of silent growth that the world can't see, because it doesn't happen in public. It occurs in your notebooks, in your long walks, in the hours spent reworking the same sentence, system, or structure until something clicks.

To be strategically obsessed is to fall out of love with novelty. Not because you're slow or outdated, but because you understand what novelty hides. It's often a mask for avoidance. A way to delay real work by constantly chasing a fresh context. The new project. The new opportunity. The new idea. But each time you chase the new, you reset the clock. You forfeit the traction you had. You start over, over and over again.

Depth, on the other hand, compounds. Every pass you take at the same problem becomes sharper. Every version gets closer. You start seeing patterns others miss. You begin to feel the material, the idea, the system, like a craftsman who knows when the wood is going to split before it makes a sound. You develop intuition, not because you're lucky, but because you stayed. You endured the boredom long enough to reach the intelligence on the other side.

People crave mastery, but they're allergic to repetition. They want results without monotony. But repetition is the forge. It's where depth is earned. Anyone can make a splash. Few can make an impact. Obsession chooses impact.

This is where strategic obsession diverges from romanticized hustle. You're not chasing inputs. You're not glorifying 18-hour workdays or frenzied output. You're crafting depth. You're making something that only becomes obvious after the hundredth iteration, not the first. And that's hard. Because there's very little external validation in those middle chapters. No one claps for refinement. But refinement is where greatness lives.

The problem with novelty is that it resets your learning curve. Every time you jump to a new platform, model, niche, or skill, you restart at zero. That might feel invigorating at first. But it's a trap. Because novelty fools you into thinking progress is being made, when really, you're just repeating the beginner cycle endlessly. Actual progress is nonlinear. It gets ugly. It stalls. It demands that you go backward before you leap forward. And you'll never experience that trajectory if you keep chasing something shiny.

Obsession teaches you to stay. To sit with friction. To push through plateaus instead of abandoning them. It redefines progress as depth, not variety. And in doing so, it makes you powerful in an invisible way, until it isn't.

One of the most valuable things obsession gives you is internal pacing. You stop needing the dopamine of quick wins because you start to trust the slow burn. You begin to feel the shape of your work, not just its speed. You stop asking, "Is this still exciting?" and start asking, "Is this still *true*?" That shift is the difference between impulse and purpose.

Depth gives you leverage. With depth, a single insight can unlock ten years of results. Without it, you spend ten years chasing insights that never add up to anything substantial. Most people live in the shallows, busy, stimulated, reactive. They don't even know what depth feels like. They've never stayed with one question, one craft, one vision long enough to find out.

But you're not most people. If you're reading this, it's because some part of you already suspects that the shallow game is rigged. The real advantage comes not from being the fastest to adapt, but from being the one who doesn't need to.

Depth isn't a lifestyle. It's a strategic choice. A refusal to abandon meaning for motion. A conscious decision to focus not on how much you can consume, but how deeply you can understand, refine, and execute the thing that matters most.

Chapter 4: Strategic vs. Stubborn

There's a fine line between obsession and delusion. That line is a strategy.

To the outside world, obsession can look like stubbornness. You're saying no to obvious shortcuts. You're rejecting advice. You're continuing to work on something long after others would have pivoted or walked away. But there's a difference, an important one. Stubbornness is emotional. It's about pride, ego, or fear of change. Strategy, on the other hand, is intentional. It's based on clarity, data, and vision. And if you want to turn obsession into a competitive advantage, you have to learn the difference.

Stubbornness resists change because change threatens identity. Strategic obsession embraces change when it serves the mission. It's not afraid to kill ideas, shift tactics, or redesign systems. But it never abandons the core. The direction remains fixed, even if the methods evolve. That's the difference between spinning your wheels and sharpening your edge.

There's a kind of pride in being "the person who never gives up." But not all persistence is wise. The question isn't whether you can endure. It's whether your endurance is aimed at something worth striving for. Stubbornness keeps you stuck. Strategy keeps you aligned.

It's easy to romanticize grit. Our culture worships the image of the lone genius grinding through the night. But obsession doesn't mean ignoring reality. It means responding to it *intelligently*. You stay in the game, yes, but not in the same position forever. Strategic obsessives iterate. They don't just push harder; they push smarter.

The danger with obsession is that it can become blind. You fall so in love with your idea, your process, your version of the story that you stop seeing the terrain. You ignore signals. You reject feedback. You start defending the structure instead of defending the mission. That's when obsession slips into dysfunction.

But strategy brings perspective. It creates checkpoints. You don't measure your conviction by how hard you work; you measure it by how you're thinking. A stubborn mind is closed. A strategic mind is committed *and* adaptive. That tension is where real power lives.

One of the hallmarks of strategic obsession is the willingness to change everything *except* the mission. You rewire your habits, your calendar, your workflows, even your metrics. You test assumptions. You take feedback seriously. But you don't let that feedback pull you off course. You don't abandon the mountain just because the path got harder.

The challenge is that from the outside, strategic obsession looks slow. It doesn't pivot constantly. It doesn't make grand gestures. It doesn't chase the spotlight. It moves with deliberation. And in a world that values hype over patience, that makes you look stubborn. So be it. You're not here for their approval. You're here to build something they don't understand yet.

Even inside your mind, the difference can blur. When things get hard, and they will, it's tempting to justify stagnation as commitment. You tell yourself you're staying the course when, in reality, you're avoiding the discomfort of re-evaluation. That's when you need to ask: Am I protecting the mission, or protecting my pride?

Strategic obsessives build feedback loops into their process, not just to get better, but to stay honest. They check for signs of drift. They seek out friction. They don't wait until everything breaks to make adjustments. And when they do adjust, they do it ruthlessly. Not to please others, but to remove what no longer serves the endgame.

You can be flexible without being scattered. You can be adaptable without being aimless. The key is to anchor your flexibility in something larger than your mood. Something that remains constant despite the market's fluctuations. That's what makes it strategic. That's what makes it sustainable.

The world will always try to push you off course. Some of those pushes will come disguised as good advice. Others will come wrapped in fear, yours or someone else's. But strategy means you've already chosen your compass. You don't need to re-decide your direction every time the wind shifts. You adjust your sails.

There's an integrity to strategic obsession. A calm, unshakeable knowing. Not loud. Not reactive. Just aligned. That's what separates it from the raw, brittle energy of stubbornness. One resists because one is afraid to be wrong. The other persists because it knows it's right, even if the world hasn't caught up yet.

You don't need to defend your pace, your process, or your focus. Let others misunderstand you. Let them mislabel it as resistance. You're not stuck. You're deliberate. You're not inflexible. You're precise.

And when you do break something, change something, or walk away from something, let it be for one reason only: because the strategy demands it. Not because you got tired. Not because someone doubted you. And not because the work got quiet.

Quiet is where obsession finds its edge.

Chapter 5: Why You're Not Distracted

You're not as distracted as you think you are. You're undecided.

Distraction gets blamed for everything. You can't finish a project; it must be the phone. You can't sit down to write; it must be the notifications. You scroll too much, toggle too often, and procrastinate too hard; it must be the algorithm. But here's the uncomfortable truth: distraction is usually a symptom, not a cause. When you haven't fully decided what matters, everything feels like an interruption. When you know exactly what you're here to do, most of the noise fades by itself.

The world isn't any noisier than it was last year. It's just that most people haven't chosen what to care about. That's why every ping pulls them in. They're not distracted, they're uncommitted—and uncommitted minds chase stimulation as a substitute for direction.

Obsession ends that indecision. It draws a line. It says: This is the mission. Everything else is background radiation. Obsession doesn't mean you never get interrupted; it means you know what to return to. The difference is that you've already decided. You're not scanning. You're not wondering. You're not endlessly evaluating your next move. You're moving.

Strategic obsession is the cure for chronic indecision. It removes 99% of the mental overhead that comes from asking, "What should I be doing right now?" The answer is: the work. Not the inbox. Not the podcast. Not the comment thread. The work.

When you don't decide, your brain decides for you, and it picks the path of least resistance. That means scrolling instead of thinking, and checking instead of building, and reacting instead of creating. It's not because you're lazy. It's because you're lost in ambiguity. You haven't put a flag in the ground. You haven't made the decision that lets all the other choices go.

We talk about distraction like it's a personal failing. But in reality, most distractions are environmental. Your phone isn't the problem; your lack of clarity is. Obsessives get distracted too. But they come back faster. They're pulled back by gravity. Because they've already committed, they've already defined the center of their map.

The people who seem most focused aren't running on discipline; they're running on decision. They've structured their world so that attention flows naturally toward the mission. That structure isn't rigid. It's responsive. But it's also intentional. They don't rely on willpower to stay on track. They rely on architecture.

Undecided people try to out-hustle their uncertainty. They add tools, systems, routines, anything to fight the chaos. But it's not a productivity problem. It's a conviction problem. You don't need a new framework. You need a commitment.

Obsession is that commitment. It's the filter that makes all the little choices easy. You don't have to debate how to spend the next hour. You don't have to guess what deserves your energy. You already know. Because you've already decided, and that decision frees up enormous cognitive space.

This doesn't mean your direction never changes. It means you stop pretending you don't have one. You stop hedging your bets.

You stop showing up with one foot in and one foot out. You stop wasting energy on what-ifs. The decision to go all in on one mission removes hundreds of smaller decisions that used to slow you down.

When you know what you're obsessed with, most of life gets simpler. Not easier, but simpler. Your schedule simplifies. Your inputs are narrow. Your to-do list reflects the changes you tolerate. Who you listen to changes. What you measure changes. Because your life is no longer organized around optionality. It's organized around an outcome.

You can't out-hack a lack of obsession. You can't systematize your way out of strategic doubt. If you don't know what you're building, it won't matter how well you organize your time. The enemy isn't a distraction. It's ambiguity. The solution isn't silence. It's clarity.

So decide. Not later. Not when things are less chaotic. Not after you buy another course or read another book. Now. Decide what deserves your full bandwidth. Decide what's worth enduring for. Decide what you're willing to look foolish for, suffer for, get bored with, and still come back to day after day.

And then, and this is the part that most people miss, you must *re-decide* every day.

Clarity is not a one-time event. It's not a tattoo. It's a practice. It's something you reaffirm through your actions, schedule, and boundaries. Obsession is not immune to drift. You don't just commit once and coast. You commit again and again, in the face of doubt, boredom, and opportunity. That's what makes it powerful. That's what makes it rare.

The world is full of smart, talented people who never do anything significant because they never fully decide. They hedge. They dabble. They pivot at the first sign of discomfort. And they wonder why nothing sticks.

The ones who win don't just choose their path. They *close the others*. They burn the "maybes" and commit to saying yes with their whole life. That's not recklessness. That's resolved.

You're not distracted. You just haven't finished deciding.

Chapter 6: Time Isn't Running Out

You tell yourself that time is running out, that you should be further ahead. That you're behind schedule, behind your peers, behind the version of yourself you imagined by now. And so you panic. You pivot. You try to make up for lost ground by rushing forward, anywhere, so long as it feels like motion.

But the truth is, you're not out of time. You're just out of alignment.

Time doesn't move faster because you're anxious. It doesn't punish you for missing a milestone. It just passes. Neutral. Steady. Indifferent. The panic you feel isn't a response to time; it's a response to drift. A life that feels scattered, unanchored, and out of sync with what you know you should be doing. When you're on track, really on track, time slows down. You don't feel rushed. You feel *aimed*.

The modern world has confused urgency with importance. We're told to act quickly, decide now, and accelerate always. But what happens when you accelerate in the wrong direction? You don't just waste time, you compound failure. Rushing is not the cure for regret. Alignment is.

When you're strategically obsessed, time stops being the enemy. It becomes the ally. You stop counting how much you have left and start using what's right in front of you. You measure progress not in hours worked or boxes checked, but in how close you're getting to the real thing, the mission, the outcome, the version of the work that only obsession makes possible.

It's easy to compare your timeline to someone else's. To see their press release, their exit, their book launch, and their followers, and feel like you're late. But you're not on their path. You're not building what they're building. You're not chasing what they're chasing. Obsession frees you from that timeline. It grounds you in your own.

Being behind is a feeling, not a fact. It's the result of having a goal but no system. A desire but no commitment. A sense of urgency but no direction. Once you find the right track, your track, you realize how much time you have. And how much you wasted worrying about a race you were never meant to run.

Your obsession doesn't need to speed up. It needs to *be rooted*. The goal isn't to catch up. It's to go deep. To make every minute count, not by filling it, but by aligning it. You don't win by moving faster; you win by driving better.

There's a difference between pace and pressure. Strategic obsession removes pressure and replaces it with pace. Pressure comes from outside expectations. Pace comes from internal rhythm. You can work hard without feeling rushed. You can be intense without being frantic. That's what obsession teaches you: how to stretch time by removing everything that wastes it.

You've been told that you need to "hurry up and matter." But that's not how anything meaningful is built. What matters takes time. Time to refine. Time to rework. Time to let complexity reveal its structure. The people who seem ahead often aren't; they're just louder. The ones who last are the ones who keep going long after the noise dies down.

If you feel like you're running out of time, ask yourself: what clock are you using? Who built it? Who decided what "on time" means? Most of the standards you've inherited are imaginary. They were created by people optimizing for speed, not depth. Their urgency is not your obligation.

Strategic obsession requires a different clock. One calibrated not by quarterly goals or viral moments, but by long arcs. Deep mastery. Asymmetric returns. You can't rush a system designed to compound slowly. And you don't need to. Because when the results come, they come all at once.

When you're aligned, your time becomes frictionless. You don't waste hours fighting yourself, trying to generate motivation from nothing. You know why you're doing what you're doing. That knowing smooths the path. It makes time feel expansive, not because the clock changes, but because *you* do.

There's a hidden cost to thinking you're behind: it makes you desperate. Desperation invites short-term thinking. It seduces you with shortcuts, distractions, and compromises. You start asking, "What's fast?" instead of "What's right?" You trade trajectory for tempo. But if your direction is wrong, faster is worse.

The truth is that obsession only works in long timeframes. It's a bet on depth. A wager that you'll gain more leverage by staying on track for ten years than by pivoting ten times. But to make that bet, you have to be willing to feel "behind" for a long time. You have to be okay with being underestimated, ignored, or overlooked. Because obsession is quiet at first, it looks slow. Until it doesn't.

Eventually, your depth catches up with you. You become undeniable. Not because you rushed, but because you stayed. The time you thought you lost wasn't lost. It was building something invisible. And one day, that invisible work becomes visible all at once.

You're not out of time. You were just off-track. Get back in alignment, and time becomes your ally again.

Chapter 7: Addiction to the Pivot

There's a moment in every journey where doubt disguises itself as strategy. When you hit a wall, experience a setback, or fail to see immediate results, your first instinct is often to change direction. You convince yourself it's adaptive. You call it responsive. You frame it as an innovative, calculated pivot. And maybe, once in a while, it is. But more often, it's not a pivot, it's an escape.

Modern culture has glamorized the pivot. In the startup world, it's practically a rite of passage. If a company changes its model, story, or market enough times, we call it agile. If an individual does it, we call them a multi-hyphenate or a creative generalist. Rarely do we ask if any of those changes were necessary, or if they provided a temporary sense of progress without the burden of follow-through. Pivoting has become a socially acceptable quitting, dressed in the language of innovation.

Obsession challenges that impulse. It does not treat friction as a signal to eject. It treats it as data to work with. A person in strategic obsession does not pivot because things are complicated, confusing, or stagnant. They pivot only when the mission demands a new approach, not when the ego demands a new distraction.

What makes the pivot seductive is that it mimics progress. A pivot feels active. You get to redesign, relaunch, and rethink. It creates the illusion of movement. You feel powerful because you're doing something new. You're reconfiguring, repositioning, starting fresh. But obsession isn't interested in new unless new is required. Obsession is interested in being better. And better is often found not in changing course, but in refining the one you're already on.

People don't become obsessed because it's convenient. They become obsessed because they can't look away. The idea owns them. It holds their attention past the point of boredom, past resistance, past external validation. That kind of fixation doesn't disappear just because a quarter didn't hit its mark, or a product flopped, or the audience wasn't ready. Obsession expects turbulence. It prepares for it. The strategically obsessed don't pivot at the first sign of discomfort; they deepen their commitment.

The cycle of constant reinvention is exhausting because it resets your momentum every time. You build, then abandon. You iterate, then discard. You tell yourself it's because the thing wasn't right. But what if it was? What if the only thing missing was duration? If every pivot costs you time, then each new direction should be held to a much higher standard than mere novelty or restlessness. Otherwise, you're not improving; you're escaping the problematic parts of mastery.

There's nothing inherently wrong with changing directions. Life and business are dynamic. The key distinction is motivation. Are you pivoting to serve the mission, or to protect your ego? Are you adjusting your method because the terrain shifted, or because the validation ran out? Strategic obsession doesn't resist change; it simply filters it. It applies pressure and inquiry before taking action. It's not reactive. It's deliberate.

The addiction to the pivot comes from a fear of being wrong. If you never stay with anything long enough to test it, then you never have to confront its failure. You can remain in permanent beta, always tweaking, constantly refining, never launching fully. It feels safe. But safety and progress rarely coexist. Obsession forces you out of that loop by requiring you to commit. Not unthinkingly, but intelligently. You commit with your eyes open and your feedback channels active. You don't cling to a broken system. But you don't run from one that's simply inconvenient.

Strategic obsession is allergic to premature exits. It does not reward compulsive reinvention. It respects timing and tests reality, but it places a premium on continuity. Because in the long game, continuity compounds in a way that chaos never can. A thousand hours spread across ten projects will rarely outperform a thousand hours poured into one. It's not just about depth; it's about duration inside that depth.

To reject the pivot is not to reject evolution. It's to reject false urgency. It's to recognize that most pivots are not driven by mission-critical intelligence, but by emotional fatigue. The truly strategic mind can feel fatigue and still stay the course. Not because it's easier, but because it's more coherent. Because the cost of starting over again and again is far greater than the temporary discomfort of sticking through a difficult stretch.

When you embrace obsession, you replace the dopamine of novelty with the discipline of consistency. You learn to work with problems instead of fleeing from them. You build things that can withstand disappointment, delay, and doubt. And eventually, you start to experience breakthroughs that only occur after long periods of apparent stagnation. These are not pivots. These are inflection points, earned through endurance, not clever branding.

What looks like stuckness from the outside is often concentration from within. To those addicted to constant change, the look of being slow, rigid, or outdated can be perceived as being obsessed. But they're not watching closely enough. What's happening is a focus that is sustained, directional, and layered. It's the kind of focus that doesn't just build something new. It creates something no one else would have had the patience to finish.

Chapter 8: The Dangers of Infinite Browsing

The modern mind is drowning in options. We have more information than we can ever process, more content than we can ever consume, and more opportunities than we can meaningfully pursue. It feels like power. It feels like freedom. But infinite choice has a cost, and that cost is depth.

Infinite browsing is a state of suspended focus. You're not building. You're not committing. You're hovering. You jump from article to article, idea to idea, niche to niche, hoping something will click. You're researching, comparing, and exploring. But what you're not doing is deciding. And that's the danger. Because the more you browse, the more you normalize indecision. It starts to feel productive when it's paralyzed.

The internet has given us a simulation of progress. Every scroll delivers the dopamine of discovery. Every click feels like motion. But beneath that surface-level activity is a stalled engine. Obsession can't survive in that environment. It needs you to choose. It needs friction, boundaries, and sustained attention. None of which exists in the culture of infinite browsing.

Strategic obsession doesn't reject research. It uses research for a purpose. It doesn't binge ideas, it integrates them. There's a vast difference between reading ten essays on a subject and applying one of them so thoroughly that it reshapes your approach. Infinite browsing accumulates inputs. Obsession converts them.

There's a false safety in staying in research mode. It allows you to feel engaged without being exposed. As long as you're still "learning," no one can challenge the quality of your work, because there is no work yet. You're always preparing and constantly refining. Always not quite ready. But readiness doesn't come from more input. It comes from action.

One of the most evident signs that you're in infinite browsing mode is the endless creation of alternate paths. You start five outlines but finish none. You brainstorm new angles instead of testing the original one. You pivot at the point of friction instead of pushing through. Obsession forces you to close doors, not open more of them. It's not about narrowing possibilities because you're afraid. It's about narrowing them because you're focused.

The longer you stay in the browsing phase, the harder it is to leave. You become habituated to surface-level thinking. You start to fear commitment because it means sacrificing the endless potential of all those other options. But potential is only valuable when it becomes actual. Strategic obsession takes the risk of choosing one direction and riding it out, knowing that depth will eventually outpace optionality.

The mind, when constantly stimulated, loses its capacity for original thought. It begins to mirror the inputs it consumes. Infinite browsing creates mental noise. Obsession creates a signal. You can't hear your strategy if your brain is echoing everyone else's ideas.

There's an identity cost to infinite browsing. You begin to mistake curiosity for conviction. You start to believe that the breadth of what you know compensates for the lack of what you've built. But obsession doesn't ask what you see, it asks what

42

you've done with what you know. You can't think your way into mastery. You have to execute.

Strategic obsession is not allergic to learning. It thrives on it. But it uses learning in service of a goal, not as a goal in itself. You don't need to know everything. You need to know enough to move. You don't need to read another fifty articles. You need to sit down and apply the insight from the five you have already read.

Information is not your enemy. But saturation is. The real danger is that you drown in knowledge without building anything solid. That you collect insights like souvenirs but never stay in one place long enough to call it home. Infinite browsing fragments your attention. Obsession consolidates it.

You will always have more tabs open than time. There will always be another opinion, another framework, another trend to study. But obsession is the act of closing those tabs. Not all at once. But intentionally. You prune the noise, so the signal has space to grow.

This doesn't mean you reject the world. It means you reject the illusion that consuming it all will somehow prepare you. It won't. You get prepared by doing. By starting before you're ready. By committing before you're certain. And by staying long enough with a single pursuit to become irreplaceable within it.

There is no breakthrough at the bottom of another scroll. There is no mastery in endless research. At some point, you stop gathering and start shaping. At some point, you stop browsing and start building. That shift is the inflection point between interest and obsession. It's the moment when you decide that your mind isn't just a container, it's a forge. And what you build inside it will only matter if you allow yourself to stay.

The greatest thinkers, builders, and creators did not get where they are because they had access to better information. They arrived there by stopping consumption and starting to refine. They stopped hopping between trends and gave one pursuit enough oxygen to breathe, evolve, and grow. You can't compound clarity if you're constantly resetting your focus.

Every obsession starts with a period of gathering. But it only becomes strategic when the gathering ends and the commitment begins. So, ask yourself, what are you still browsing for? And what are you willing to stop browsing long enough to build?

Chapter 9: Identity as a Weapon, Not a Crutch

Identity is one of the most powerful tools in the strategic obsessive's arsenal, but only when used with intention. If you don't define your identity, it will define you. Left unchecked, identity becomes a cage. It hardens into performance. You become what others expect, rather than what your obsession demands. But when wielded correctly, identity becomes a focusing mechanism. It amplifies your trajectory, aligns your behavior, and removes the ambiguity that drains your energy.

In a distracted world, identity is a filter. When you know who you are and what you're building, the noise becomes easier to ignore. You stop trying to be everything for everyone. You stop chasing every opportunity, responding to every signal, and reinventing yourself for every platform. Identity helps you say no, not because you're rigid, but because you're clear.

But clarity takes work. Most people build their identity from the outside in. They look for belonging before direction. They wait for validation before committing to a path. That makes them reactive. They adapt to the environment instead of shaping it. But obsession flips that logic. It builds identity from the inside out. It starts with a commitment and then reshapes the world around it.

The strategic obsessive doesn't use identity as a shield. They don't use it to avoid change, feedback, or evolution. They use it to anchor themselves through change. When the feedback is harsh, the market is indifferent, or the journey is slow, identity keeps the mission intact, not through ego, but through alignment.

You don't stay committed because you're stubborn. You stay because it's who you are.

When identity becomes fused with obsession, discipline starts to feel automatic. You no longer need to "stay motivated." You're simply behaving according to your design. Decisions get easier. Doubt gets quieter. You're not negotiating with yourself every morning. You've already decided who you are, and this is what that person does.

This is the quiet power of identity: it removes the friction of indecision. It doesn't eliminate all resistance, but it narrows the path. It becomes a compass. Every opportunity, distraction, or obstacle gets evaluated through a different lens. Does this align with who I am becoming? Does this serve the mission I've committed to? If not, the answer is no.

Misused, identity becomes brittle. It becomes a performance. You start protecting the version of yourself others recognize, rather than the one that's evolving inside the work. That's when growth stalls. That's when obsession becomes performative. Strategic obsession never sacrifices evolution in the name of recognition. It lets the identity expand as the work grows.

You'll be tempted to brand yourself early. To codify your role, your reputation, your "lane" before the work has matured. But real obsession outgrows its early labels. It compels you to reconsider your perspective, upgrade your beliefs, and shed old habits. Identity, when properly constructed, isn't a costume. It's a framework. It's the architecture that supports your long-term mission, not the facade that pleases the algorithm.

Most people are afraid to lose their identity because they've mistaken it for their value. But your value doesn't come from what you call yourself. It comes from what you consistently produce. If you stop creating in service of your obsession and start performing in service of your reputation, you've traded your edge for applause. That's not identity. That's branding. And branding, when untethered from depth, is just noise.

The deeper you go into strategic obsession, the more your identity will shift. You'll outgrow the roles you started with. You'll notice your goals evolve from trophies to tools. You'll begin to seek leverage instead of applause. That transition can feel disorienting. But it's necessary. Your identity must stretch to accommodate the size of the work. If it doesn't, you'll start shrinking the work to fit the comfort of the identity.

Obsession, at its best, is a form of self-authoring. You are not waiting to be discovered. You are declaring yourself into existence. You are saying, "This is who I am, and this is the thing I will build, whether you understand it or not." That level of conviction is magnetic, not because it's loud, but because it's earned.

Your job is not to explain your identity to the world. Your job is to live it so consistently that the world adapts around it. That doesn't mean you ignore feedback or resist iteration. It means your core is anchored. You can adapt tactics without diluting your purpose. You can evolve your methods without compromising your values.

A well-constructed identity becomes a form of leverage. It builds trust. It signals consistency. It attracts the right people and repels the wrong ones. Over time, it creates a gravitational field around your work. People don't just follow what you do; they align with what you represent.

But that leverage only compounds if it's real. And real identity is lived, not declared. It's visible in how you spend your time, how you make decisions, and what you're willing to walk away from. It's not your bio. It's your behaviour. And it should always be shaped by the work, not the other way around.

Chapter 10: Thinking in Decades

Most people think in days. A few think in months. Some believe in years. Almost no one thinks in decades. That's because thinking in decades feels impossible. It's too big, too vague, too uncertain. The world changes too fast. The variables are infinite. And yet, that kind of long-range thinking is the exact foundation that obsession needs to compound properly.

When you think in decades, everything changes. The way you measure progress changes. The way you react to setbacks changes. The urgency drops, but the gravity increases. You stop chasing novelty and start seeking alignment. The question becomes less about how fast you can build and more about how long it can last. You begin to shift from sprint metrics to legacy metrics.

Strategic obsession isn't about scale for the sake of growth. It's about duration, resilience, and inevitability. It asks whether the work you're doing today has the strength to survive ten years of pressure, iteration, and reinvention. That's not a question most people ask. They're too busy optimizing for the week, chasing attention, and pleasing stakeholders. But obsession doesn't live in short-term optimization. It lives in long-term coherence.

Thinking in decades forces a higher standard. You stop making decisions based on convenience and start making them based on consequence. You design systems with future friction in mind. You're not just managing today's workload; you're preparing for the weight of tomorrow's scale. You trade dopamine for durability. And in doing so, you build structures that don't collapse under scrutiny.

This isn't about predicting the future. It's about preparing for it. You can't know what will happen, but you can see who you intend to become. That's the anchor. Long-term obsession is less about goals and more about direction. You're not forecasting outcomes, you're committing to a trajectory. You are shaping yourself into the kind of person who could withstand a decade-long journey with clarity and fire intact.

When you stretch your timeline, your tolerance expands with it. Minor failures become just that, minor. Delays become tolerable. Detours become part of the design. The pressure to perform right now fades, and in its place grows a pressure to remain aligned. You're no longer trying to win the moment. You're trying to stay relevant through many of them.

Obsession gives you something to evolve around. It's the spine of your decade. Without it, you drift. You say yes to things that dilute your focus. You respond to pressures that break your rhythm. But when you're thinking in decades, every "yes" has a long shadow. You start to measure trade-offs differently. You begin to say no from a place of future integrity, not present convenience.

Most people aren't lazy. They're compressed. Their vision is so small that there's no room to grow inside it. They work hard on tiny cycles, never seeing that the work could be bigger than the moment. Thinking in decades gives your effort room to breathe. You stop feeling behind because you're finally operating on a scale that makes your ambition feel proportional to your potential.

Of course, long-term thinking has risks. It invites procrastination. It can mask avoidance. But strategic obsession adds urgency to that scale. It grounds the decade in daily action. You are not just dreaming about ten years from now, you're building the daily momentum that earns it. You're reverse-engineering a legacy, not fantasizing about one.

It also clarifies priorities. If something won't matter in ten years, it likely doesn't deserve ten hours. That's not always easy to accept. Urgency seduces. Short-term validation feels good. But obsession gives you a different kind of reward, the quiet power of knowing you're working on something that can't be taken away, even if it isn't understood yet.

Obsession over time becomes identity. And identity over time becomes culture. If you're building something that's meant to outlive your direct involvement, then thinking in decades isn't just a mindset, it's a requirement. You can't build institutions, movements, or empires with a quarterly brain. You have to zoom out far enough to see beyond the present noise.

There's a reason so few people operate this way. Long-term thinking is lonely. It's often misunderstood. It's hard to measure. It doesn't perform well on social media. But the ones who do it, quietly, methodically, are the ones who reshape the playing field. They're not optimizing for views. They're optimizing for volume. And volume takes time.

Thinking in decades doesn't mean waiting ten years to start. It means doing today's work in a way that still makes sense ten years from now. It means choosing principles that won't expire. It means treating time as an asset to be invested, not a threat to outrun.

If you can hold that frame, everything sharpens. You stop reacting to the week's chaos. You start building for the century. You realize that progress isn't about how much ground you cover; it's about whether you're even on the correct map. Thinking in decades pulls you out of comparison. It recalibrates your ambition. It makes you braver. And it makes you more patient.

When others burn out from chasing trends, you'll still be building. When others pivot to keep up, you'll already be ahead, not because you moved faster, but because you moved better. That's what obsession over time gives you: not just results but results that last.

Chapter 11: The System Behind the Obsession

Obsession without a system is a bonfire. It burns hot and fast, but it can't sustain. You may feel inspired, driven, alive with vision, but if you don't build infrastructure around that energy, it dissipates. Strategic obsession requires scaffolding. It demands structure that doesn't stifle intensity but channels it. Without a system, your obsession becomes a cycle of bursts and breakdowns.

People assume that obsession is chaotic by nature. They picture the frenzied artist, the sleepless founder, the relentless athlete grinding toward some invisible edge. But the most enduring obsession isn't wild, it's methodical. It's not fueled by mood. It's driven by rhythm. That rhythm is built through systems.

A system, in this context, is not software. It's not productivity hacks. It's not even a strict routine. A system is the environment, process, and accountability framework that enables your obsession to thrive in real life. It's the calendar decisions, the cognitive filters, the physical and mental architecture you construct to make your vision executable. Systems don't replace obsession; they make it sustainable.

Without a system, every day is a decision. Should I work today? For how long? On what? Where do I start? What matters most? That constant negotiation is exhausting. It drains cognitive bandwidth that should be spent on building, thinking, and executing. The system removes that ambiguity. It frontloads the structure so you can focus on the work itself, rather than navigating how to do it.

The most powerful systems are simple, but sacred. They're built around clarity. They ask: what do I need to be doing, when do I need to do it, and how do I keep doing it when motivation fades? They answer those questions not with inspiration, but with design.

Obsession is not about intensity. It's about consistency. Intensity happens in spikes. It's easy to get hyped for a week. But an obsession that wins over decades requires consistency, and consistency is built by systems that remove friction. Friction isn't just an inconvenience; it's the enemy of momentum. Your system exists to minimize it.

There is no single system that works for everyone. Some obsessives thrive with rigid schedules, others with creative sprints. Some use elaborate trackers; others live out of notebooks. The format doesn't matter. What matters is alignment. The system must serve the obsession, not the other way around. When your system is built around the wrong metrics or borrowed templates, it becomes a trap. It begins to distract you from your mission instead of drawing you toward it.

You will be tempted to keep redesigning your system instead of using it. That's one of the quiet threats to long-term obsession: constant optimization becomes a form of avoidance. You tweak, upgrade, and restructure not because it improves the work, but because it gives you the illusion of control. A sound system is invisible when it's working. It disappears into the rhythm of your day, like a road that lets you drive without thinking about the asphalt.

Strategic obsession treats systems as support beams, not cages. The goal is not to automate your creativity, but to protect the conditions where it thrives. That means setting boundaries around time, inputs, rest, and focus. It means giving your future self fewer chances to opt out, give up, or defer. The system doesn't eliminate resistance. It reduces the number of excuses that get in your way.

It's important to understand that your system is a living thing. It will evolve as you grow. What works in year one might fail in year five. The nature of your work, your resources, and your constraints will all shift. Strategic obsession expects this. It doesn't cling to the system as an identity. It iterates. But it never abandons structure altogether. The commitment is to rhythm, not rigidity.

This is where many people fall apart. They believe that obsession means working harder. But real obsession works smarter. It designs repeatable patterns. It uses automation where possible. It protects deep work. It builds in reflection. The most strategically obsessed individuals are often the most systematized, not because they love structure, but because they refuse to leave their progress up to mood.

A system creates feedback loops. You can measure your consistency. You can track your lagging metrics and leading indicators. You can identify bottlenecks. This turns your obsession from a feeling into a machine. It doesn't dehumanize the work; it amplifies your capacity to deliver it. You become reliable. Predictable. Not to others, but to yourself.

Systems also protect your obsession from burnout. They build in recovery. They create whitespace. They make sure the machine doesn't run so hot that it burns itself out. Obsession without breaks is not noble; it's unsustainable. The system makes your obsession livable. It's what allows you to stay in the game long enough to matter.

No great work has ever been built on the back of willpower alone. What separates those who finish from those who fade is not the strength of their feelings, but the strength of their systems. Systems absorb inconsistency. They protect momentum during personal storms. They allow for recovery without collapse. They don't care how inspired you feel on a given day; they exist to carry you through.

When obsession meets a system that's well-built and frequently refined, the results compound in silence. There are no dramatic starts and stops. Just consistent, daily execution that adds up over time into something undeniable. And that's the real goal: not to burn brightly and disappear, but to burn steadily and reshape the landscape.

Chapter 12: Discipline Is the Shortcut

Discipline is rarely glamorous. It doesn't trend on social media. It doesn't produce immediate applause. It is quiet, repetitive, and often invisible. And yet, for those serious about long-term impact, discipline is the only real shortcut. While others are looking for hacks, shortcuts, or inspiration, the strategically obsessed commit to process. They don't wait to feel like it. They design their life around doing it anyway.

Discipline shrinks the distance between effort and result. Most people waste energy negotiating with themselves: Should I do this now or later? Should I skip today and double up tomorrow? Should I restructure my system? Should I pivot again? Discipline closes those loops. It makes the decision once and then honours it. It doesn't re-litigate every morning. It moves.

The myth that discipline is about restriction misses the point entirely. Proper discipline is about liberation. It frees you from the tyranny of mood. It gives you the ability to act regardless of your emotional weather. That's not robotic, it's strategic. Mood is unpredictable. Progress requires predictability. Obsession becomes sustainable only when it's fortified by discipline.

You don't need to be the most talented. You don't need to be the most connected. But if you are the most consistent, you will pass most people in time. The marketplace is filled with abandoned projects, half-built ideas, and enthusiastic starters. Very few people finish. Discipline is what bridges the excitement of the beginning with the satisfaction of completion.

For the strategically obsessed, discipline is not about grinding harder than everyone else. It's about staying in rhythm when others fall out. It's about showing up, doing the work, and leaving nothing to chance. You don't need to be motivated; you need to be consistent. You don't need a spark, you need a system. And that system lives and dies on discipline.

People think they're stuck because they don't have the right strategy. Often, they're just undisciplined. They don't stick with one direction long enough to let the strategy reveal its compounding effects. They change their goals every few weeks. They chase the following shiny framework. They confuse movement with progress. But motion without direction is waste, and direction without discipline is still just theory.

One of the most significant lies of the modern age is that discipline kills creativity. In truth, discipline is what protects it. Without discipline, your mind is in constant triage. You're reacting, responding, recalibrating every day. That leaves no room for deep work. Creativity needs constraints. It needs a container. It requires the discipline of commitment to go from idea to execution.

You don't become great by doing extraordinary things once in a while. You become great by doing ordinary things every day with exceptional consistency. Discipline turns the mundane into leverage. It transforms the boring into the breakthrough. That's the real secret behind elite performance. Not magic. Not luck. Just the relentless application of pressure, day after day, long after others would have quit.

There's a moment in every journey when motivation vanishes. The novelty wears off. The applause slows down. The results take longer than expected. That's where most people turn back. That's where they say, "Maybe this isn't for me." But the obsessed push through. Not because they feel like it, but because they have already decided. That decision is discipline. It's the muscle that keeps you moving when emotion fails.

Discipline is the proof that you're serious. Anyone can be passionate. Passion is easy. It's fun to talk about, easy to post about, and quick to ignite. But it burns out fast. Discipline is different. It's not about how loud your ambition is. It's about how quietly and consistently you execute when nobody's watching.

The world is full of talented people who have never shipped. Smart people who never shipped. Creative people who never shipped. Discipline is the difference between intention and impact. Between theory and traction. Between ideas and assets. It doesn't care about your potential. It cashes out only what you prove.

If you want to be strategically obsessed, you must train yourself to act when it's hard. That doesn't mean pushing through illness or denying your limits. It means refusing to let inconvenience be an excuse. It means honouring the plan you made when you were clear-headed, not renegotiating it every time the work gets uncomfortable. Strategic obsession doesn't avoid friction. It budgets for it.

And here's the paradox: the more disciplined you become, the less effort discipline requires. It turns into identity. You stop thinking of it as effortful. It's just who you are now. You don't need tricks to stay on track; you've built a track that fits your momentum. You've shaped your environment to support the behaviour. That's what mature discipline looks like: not more complex work, but fewer escape routes.

Discipline is also infectious. When others see it in you, it creates a gravitational pull. It signals credibility. It earns trust. People start to believe in your work not because of your pitch, but because of your posture. They trust what you've built because they've seen how you create. This is the quiet advantage of the disciplined mind; it inspires belief without needing to demand it.

The most disciplined people aren't cold. They aren't mechanical. They're committed. They've chosen a path, and they've decided to become the kind of person who honours that path regardless of circumstance. That commitment shows up not in grand gestures but in small consistencies: the unskipped day, the final edit, the avoided distraction. And over time, those tiny wins stack into legacy.

You don't have to love discipline to benefit from it. You only have to respect what it makes possible. Obsession without discipline is a fire without a furnace. It flares up, then fades. But an obsession grounded in discipline becomes durable. Reliable. Unstoppable.

And that is the ultimate shortcut, because while others burn out chasing sparks, you'll be building something that lasts.

Chapter 13: The Loneliness of the Focused

Focus doesn't just narrow your field of vision; it narrows your field of belonging. When you choose obsession, you decide to walk a path fewer people understand. You start saying no more than you say yes. You begin to ignore what others obsess over. The more focused you become, the more invisible you feel, not because you're lost, but because you've stopped broadcasting your distractions.

There is a loneliness that comes with this. Not everyone can walk with you. Not everyone will even want to. Most people need constant engagement, mutual validation, and social proof. They want to belong in the moment, to trend with the group, to remain visible. But focus takes you away from the crowd. Strategic obsession demands it. You cannot stay tethered to everything and expect to delve deeply into anything.

This is the first significant cost of deep work: social dissonance. You stop attending events. You respond late to texts. You miss birthdays. You withdraw from group chats. And people notice. They assume you're drifting. They worry, or worse, resent. But you're not lost, you're aligned. You've stopped apologizing for your priorities.

The world doesn't reward this behaviour immediately. It resists it. It punishes silence with obscurity. It shames intensity with accusations of imbalance. When you're focused, you threaten those who aren't. You become a mirror, and not everyone likes what they see. This creates subtle pressure to dilute. To prove you're still social. To show up just enough to seem normal. But focus and normal rarely coexist.

The truth is, loneliness isn't just a byproduct of focus; it's a feature. It's the crucible where clarity forms. When the noise drops out, your real questions surface. Your motivations get tested. Your identity gets exposed. You find out whether your obsession is strong enough to survive without applause. That's when it deepens. That's when it becomes real.

Strategic obsession doesn't demand isolation, but it does require selectivity. You don't cut out people to be cold. You cut out distractions to be clear. There is a profound difference. Focus creates emotional distance, not because you love others less, but because you've chosen to love your mission more. That tension will not be understood by most. That's okay. It's not their job to understand. It's your job to hold the line.

As your focus sharpens, your circle shrinks. This isn't a tragedy. It's a filter. Those who remain are those who understand. They don't need constant updates. They respect your discipline. They cheer you on without needing proximity. These people are rare. But they are enough. Strategic obsession doesn't require crowds. It requires conviction and the few who reinforce it.

There's also a loneliness in pace. Most people work in cycles of burn and coast. You work consistently. You don't sprint toward weekends or live for vacations. You've made your daily effort the reward. That's not glamorous. It's not shareable. It's not even visible. Which means it's often lonely. But that's also where the edge is.

Obsession doesn't ask if you're available. It asks if you're committed. It won't always feel good. There will be mornings where the silence feels sharp, where you wonder if you're missing out, where you question if anyone even notices what you're building. That's when most people pivot. They return to the noise for comfort. But those who stay in solitude find something else: power.

Solitude refines you. It removes the performative layers. It eliminates comparison. It trains you to validate from within. You stop seeking metrics for motivation. You start building for meaning. That's a shift few people make because it requires enduring the internal static long enough to hear your signal. And that signal, your signal, is the blueprint for something no one else can replicate.

Focus is a form of rebellion. It rejects the frantic urgency of everyone else's priorities. It says no to 99 things so that it can say yes with full force to one. That is threatening to those who spread themselves thin. It exposes the fragility of their commitments, which is why your focus will sometimes attract resistance. Not because you're wrong, but because you're proof that a deeper path exists.

The most outstanding work in history was born from this kind of loneliness. Not hermitage, but concentrated clarity. The refusal to dilute. The discipline to stay with a question long enough to crack it open. That doesn't happen in a room full of noise. It occurs in the quiet corners where no one claps, but something essential takes shape.

The good news is this: the loneliness of focus doesn't last forever. It evolves. As you build, others find you. The right collaborators emerge. The work becomes magnetic. People sense the weight of your intention and begin to orbit it. But that only happens if you stay the course long enough. Suppose you can hold your silence if you can resist the temptation to explain yourself too soon.

In time, focus builds gravity. What once isolated you begins to attract. The depth of your work speaks louder than your presence ever could. You no longer chase relevance; you embody it. But the transition from solitude to influence cannot be rushed. It must be earned through patience, practice, and persistence.

You must be willing to walk alone until the work becomes undeniable. That is the cost. That is the crucible. And when you emerge, not just productive but transformed, you'll realize that the loneliness of focus wasn't a punishment. It was preparation. The silence taught you to listen. The distance taught you to see. And the discipline taught you to lead.

Chapter 14: Building Unreasonable Standards

Most people build to the standard they believe they can get away with. They deliver work that is "good enough," that won't get them fired, that might impress the average person. But strategic obsession is not fueled by adequacy. It is driven by the refusal to settle. At the heart of every meaningful pursuit lies a standard that looks unreasonable to others and often feels unreasonable to you. But that's what makes it powerful. It lifts your entire arc of execution.

Unreasonable standards are not about perfectionism. They are about identity. When you raise the bar, you force yourself to evolve. You make it impossible to meet expectations with old effort. The new standard becomes a filter: for what you tolerate, what you allow into your schedule, and who you allow into your circle. It's not elitism, it's precision. Strategic obsession requires that level of selectivity because there is no surplus of time. You're either building toward your standard or away from it.

Most people don't even know what their standard is. They've never named it. They've never drawn the line between acceptable and excellent. So, they oscillate. Some days they push. Some days they coast. They rely on mood, deadlines, or pressure. But those who operate at a high level know exactly what "great" looks like for them. They see the delta between a 90 and a 98. And they don't pretend not to see it.

When you decide to build to an unreasonable standard, your work becomes uncomfortable, but also unmistakable. There's a quiet gravity to the things constructed with care. Readers can feel it. Clients can sense it. Partners can't ignore it. It shows up in the details. In the restraint. In the end. You don't need to shout to prove value. The standard communicates it for you.

This is not just about deliverables. It's about the way you move. The way you speak. The way you structure your week. High standards bleed into everything. They shape your posture. Your process. Your expectations of others. This isn't arrogance. It's alignment. Strategic obsession turns your standard into a system. It eliminates the daily debate about whether to push. There's no debate. You do what it takes.

Of course, the world doesn't make this easy. We are surrounded by systems optimized for scale, speed, and efficiency, not for depth. Most environments reward speed over thoughtfulness, and frequency over authenticity. But when you build with an unreasonable standard, you flip that. You trade speed for substance. You trade flash for foundation. It costs more upfront, but it pays dividends that no shortcut ever could.

Raising your standard isn't about doing more. It's about doing better. That often means doing less but doing it with full attention. It means cutting projects that don't meet the bar— saying no to partnerships that dilute the mission—rejecting the kind of praise that celebrates mediocrity. High standards aren't just what you chase; they're what you refuse to accept.

You will frustrate people. Some will think you're overthinking. Others will think you're difficult. That's fine. You're not building for comfort. You're building for resonance. You're not trying to be everywhere. You're trying to be undeniable where it counts. This only happens when you stop measuring your work against what's acceptable and start measuring it against what's *possible*.

The hard part is that unreasonable standards don't come with applause. No one thanks you for doing the extra draft. No one claps for the way you restructured the last 5% of a project to remove friction. But that's the point. You don't do it for attention. You do it because you've decided this is the kind of work you're going to put into the world. That internal pressure becomes your true north.

Eventually, the standard reshapes you. You begin to feel physical discomfort when things are sloppy. You start seeing details others miss. You grow intolerant of laziness, vagueness, and excuses. This doesn't make you better than others, but it does make you different. And that difference compounds. Over time, it becomes a moat not just of quality, but of trust.

Clients trust you more. Audiences feel you more. Colleagues respect you more. Not because you're loud, but because your standard is consistent. That consistency is rare. And anything rare commands attention, especially in a world drowning in shortcuts.

High standards also force reinvention. You can't hit new levels with old habits. The bar moves up, and you must rise with it. That might mean new tools, new workflows, new mentors. It might mean auditing your environment and cutting what no longer matches your ambition. Most people avoid this because it's uncomfortable. But discomfort is the cost of elevation.

What makes a standard "unreasonable" isn't that it's impossible, it's that it feels unnatural at first. You're pushing against the inertia of the acceptable. You're confronting decades of cultural messaging that tells you to aim for balance, to be realistic, to avoid being "too much." But obsession doesn't ask for balance. It asks for devotion. And devotion only thrives when it has something sacred to protect.

That sacred thing is your standard. Not someone else's benchmark. Not the market's expectations. Yours. Defined, declared, and honoured, not occasionally, but always. And when that standard lives inside everything you do, it becomes your signature. Quiet. Relentless. Unmistakable.

Chapter 15: The Compound Interest of Effort

Effort doesn't compound overnight. That's why most people abandon it too early. They expect visible returns on invisible investments. They want confirmation that their energy is working. But strategic obsession understands a more profound truth: effort compounds in silence. Its impact is slow, then sudden. And by the time it becomes evident to others, it's already inevitable.

This is the nature of compounding: small inputs, repeated consistently, create outsized results over time. The problem is that our world is wired for immediacy. We track progress hourly, celebrate milestones daily, and chase quarterly wins. But obsession plays a longer game. It understands that most of what matters cannot be measured in short bursts. It demands that you believe before the payoff. That you show up before the applause.

There is a moment in every journey where your output exceeds your outcome. You're writing more than you're selling and practicing more than you're praised. Showing up more than you're seen. And it feels like nothing is happening. But underneath, the foundation is thickening. Skills are sharpening. Credibility is forming. Trust is accruing. These are invisible assets, until they're not.

Compounding effort doesn't just build results. It builds identity. The act of returning to work each day rewires your sense of self. You begin to think of yourself as someone who does hard things. Someone who finishes. Someone who sticks. And once you identify as that kind of person, you make different choices. You no longer negotiate with your limits. You reinforce your edge.

This is why the strategically obsessed aren't always the fastest starters, but they're the last ones standing. They build not with speed, but with rhythm. They pace themselves for endurance. They invest effort even when it feels inefficient, knowing that compounding doesn't reward intensity; it rewards consistency.

We tend to overestimate what we can achieve in a week and underestimate what we can build in five years. That's the trap of urgency. It makes us chase volume instead of depth, motion instead of traction. Strategic obsession sidesteps that. It treats each day as a single deposit. Small. Specific. Sustainable. But over time, those deposits become a fortune.

What makes compounding effort so powerful is that it operates in dimensions others can't see. The time you spend mastering nuance, refining your process, and auditing your performance may not be visible externally, but it shows up in the texture of your work. You speak with more authority. You move with more certainty. You attract higher-quality opportunities not because you're lucky, but because your effort has matured.

At first, the work feels one-sided. You give more than you get. You invest in projects that don't pay. You build products no one buys. You publish ideas that go unnoticed. And every time, the voice in your head asks: "Is this worth it?" But compounding effort doesn't answer that question today. It answers in years from now, when the momentum you've built becomes self-sustaining.

70

That's the inflection point, when your effort starts to pull returns without fresh input, when your name opens doors. When your backlog sells itself. When your discipline becomes magnetic, but that point doesn't come from a breakthrough. It comes from thousands of unrewarded reps.

The most dangerous thing you can do is stop too early. Because you'll never know how close you were. Most people quit at the first sign of stagnation. But stagnation is not failure. It's incubation. It's the quiet stretch before the visible breakthrough. And if you can survive it, if you can keep working when the results slow down, you'll tap into something exponential.

Effort compounds in networks, too. The person you helped years ago suddenly introduces you to someone pivotal. The article you wrote in obscurity ends up cited by a key thinker. The process you've built for yourself serves as the foundation for a much larger system. These are nonlinear returns. They don't obey timelines. But they reward the obsessed.

Effort also compounds in perception. The more consistent you are, the more seriously people take you. They stop wondering if this is a phase and start believing it's who they are. That shift is subtle, but transformative. It moves you from hobbyist to practitioner. From dabbler to threat. From curiosity to category leader.

Eventually, your past self starts working for you. The hours you put in when no one cared, the processes you created when no one asked, the drafts you rewrote when no one was watching, they begin to create leverage. They reduce friction. They free you up to play a bigger game. And that's when you realize: the compound interest of effort isn't just about results. It's about freedom.

Freedom to create without fear. Freedom to turn down bad deals. Freedom to protect your standards. Freedom to trust your instincts. These freedoms aren't given. They're earned. And they're earned through effort no one applauded, no one tracked, no one demanded, but you did it anyway.

Obsession doesn't guarantee success. But it does guarantee progress. And over a long enough timeline, that progress stacks into something profound. Not just in what you've built, but in who you've become.

That's the final reward of compounding effort: transformation. Not overnight. Not viral. Just deliberate, quiet, undeniable change. One rep at a time.

Chapter 16: The 100-Year Lens

Most people think in weeks. A few think in years. But obsession stretches your timeline until it bends reality. Strategic obsession doesn't just extend your focus; it warps your sense of urgency. It asks: "What would this look like if I were to build it for the next 100 years?" That question isn't literal. It's philosophical. It's not about lifespan, it's about depth, scale, and commitment. Thinking in centuries forces you out of reaction mode and into creation mode. You're no longer operating for now. You're building forever.

The 100-year lens disorients the modern mind because it defies the pace of the world. We are taught to optimize for immediacy, fast wins, viral moments, and quarterly results. We build businesses for acquisition, not endurance. We write content for clicks, not timelessness. We treat attention as currency instead of treating trust as capital. The 100-year thinker sees through this. They don't move slowly. They move deliberately. Every step is calibrated for permanence.

This lens changes what you care about. You stop asking what will get you noticed and start asking what will outlast you. You stop tracking reach and start obsessing over resonance. You begin to prioritize durability in your systems, quality in your craftsmanship, and clarity in your mission. Most of all, you eliminate distractions that don't contribute to longevity. You begin to ignore opportunities that don't compound. You stop entertaining critics who won't matter in a decade. You silence the noise not because you're fragile, but because you're building something that needs silence to grow.

Obsession under this lens becomes less frantic and more spiritual. You're not trying to be famous. You're trying to be foundational. That shift makes you dangerous in a world that worships novelty. You don't pivot at every sign of resistance. You don't abandon your path just because the market hasn't validated it. You walk forward with a kind of calm madness. Because you're not chasing relevance. You're architecting legacy.

The 100-year lens forces you to slow down long enough to ask better questions. What values do I want this work to carry long after I'm gone? What systems can I build that others could inherit? What decisions today will ripple forward for generations? These are not casual questions. They are grounded ones. They help you zoom out from the daily grind and see your work as something sacred. You become less of a player and more of a steward.

And when you adopt that mindset, quality becomes inevitable. You're not trying to win the algorithm. You're trying to earn the respect of someone who may not even be born yet. You take longer to build things. You revise more. You work with a quiet tension between humility and audacity. You care more because your work isn't about you anymore. It's about time. And time respects those who respect it.

In business, this lens forces you to reject extractive tactics. It pushes you to build brands that don't just sell but serve. You start to consider how your company handles crises, how your culture will evolve in your absence, and how your decisions will impact communities that aren't even your customers yet. You start to see your work not as a sprint to capitalize, but as a lifetime experiment in contribution.

In creativity, the 100-year lens elevates your bar. You stop producing content. You start creating canon. You stop writing to be heard. You write to be re-read. You imagine your work printed on paper a hundred years from now and ask: Would I be proud of this then? If the answer is no, you go back and do it better. Not because someone told you to. But because time is watching.

The irony is that long-term obsession often produces short-term clarity. When you know where you're going, you waste less energy on detours. You say "no" faster. You align your resources better. You attract different kinds of people, those who aren't here for the spotlight, but for the stonework. And slowly, your community begins to form, not around popularity, but around principle.

Your competition shifts, too. You stop comparing yourself to peers and start comparing yourself to your potential. You stop chasing what's trending and start chasing what's true. You study not just business cases, but civilizations. You look at architecture, philosophy, and infrastructure. You try to learn from anything that has stood the test of time, not to replicate it, but to internalize what endurance demands.

This kind of thinking isn't just rare, it's uncomfortable. The market won't reward you right away. The audience won't understand you at first. You'll appear to be moving slowly as everyone else sprints. But when the dust settles, and the trends shift, and the loudest voices fall silent, your work will still be standing because you built it for time. And time doesn't rush.

The 100-year lens is not about building slower. It's about building deeper. It's not about thinking bigger. It's about thinking longer. You're not building a moment. You're building a movement. And movements require architecture. They require fidelity. They need an almost obsessive reverence for detail, process, and principle.

And if you do it right, if you're brave enough to ignore the quick win, and disciplined enough to commit to the long path, then maybe, just maybe, your work won't need your name on it to endure. It will carry its weight. It will echo through time. And it will prove that obsession, when pointed in the right direction, is not a flaw. It's a force.

Chapter 17: The Hidden Cost of Optionality

Optionality is often marketed as the crown jewel of intelligence. Keep your options open, they say. Don't commit too early. Diversify your bets. It's the language of modern efficiency, hedging, pivoting, staying "nimble." And in certain seasons of life, optionality is useful. It helps you explore when you don't yet know your path. It allows you to adapt when circumstances demand agility. But left unchecked, optionality becomes a slow poison. Strategic obsession does not thrive on open doors; it thrives on deliberate closure.

At some point, freedom stops being empowering and starts becoming paralyzing. The endless buffet of potential dilutes the only thing that makes potential real: commitment. You can't compound what you haven't chosen. You can't master what you keep one foot out of. Optionality, when indulged beyond its purpose, becomes a defence mechanism, a way to avoid the discomfort of betting on yourself.

The hidden cost of optionality is not financial. It's energetic. It splits your attention. It fragments your identity. Every "maybe" you carry siphons energy from the "hell yes" that deserves your full weight. You start living in draft mode, skimming the surface of multiple lives but never inhabiting any of them entirely. You write outlines, not manuscripts. You build decks, not companies. You rehearse conversations, never speaking the truth out loud.

Obsession requires the opposite. It demands subtraction. It asks you to prioritize possibilities. This is not about limiting your ambition; it's about focusing it. It's about deciding which game you're playing so you can win it. The person trying to be great at five things is rarely great at one. Strategic obsession forces you to choose not because the other paths aren't interesting, but because the one you've selected is sacred.

Most people don't fear commitment itself; they fear being wrong. They fear the irreversible step. The social exposure. The sunk costs. The idea of having to answer for a decision that didn't play out. So they flirt with every opportunity, hoping one will become undeniable without them having to choose. But obsession doesn't wait for certainty. It builds it. It says, "This is the hill," and then starts climbing before the crowd has even spotted the mountain.

Optionality also warps your relationship with failure. When you're fully committed, failure sharpens you. It teaches. It refines. But when you're hedging, failure becomes justification for retreat. "I never really tried," you tell yourself. "It wasn't my real focus anyway." And just like that, the cycle of self-protection repeats. You get to keep your ego, but you sacrifice your evolution.

The brutal truth is this: most of the work that changes the world — art, science, movement-building, and entrepreneurship — is the product of unreasonable commitment. Of someone saying, "This is it," and burning the alternative. That depth creates momentum. That momentum creates compounding. That compounding creates power. And that power cannot be accessed from the middle of the road.

Choosing obsession means narrowing your aperture. It means knowing that every yes is a thousand silent no's. It means turning down good ideas, sound money, and good people simply because they're not the exact right ones. And it means embracing the solitude that comes from going deep when everyone else is still trying to go wide.

Even in elite circles, you'll see people default to optionality as a disguise for ambition. They join a dozen advisory boards. They started three companies at once. They launch five social channels with six different messages. It looks impressive. It feels productive. But it's often a strategy of avoidance. A refusal to choose something that could hold them accountable. Something that might expose their limitations. Something that, even if they gave it their all, might still not be enough.

This doesn't mean you never iterate. It doesn't mean you never evolve. It means you evolve through depth, not drift. You outgrow goals by surpassing them, not by abandoning them. You stay long enough to be shaped by the work. To let it mould you, challenge you, stretch you in ways that breadth never could. Breadth feels expansive, but depth is what anchors a legacy.

Optionality also erodes credibility. When people see you constantly shifting, hedging, they stop taking you seriously. The market respects conviction. Audiences follow clarity. Partners trust decisiveness. No one is inspired by someone who waits for a guarantee. If you want to build a reputation that magnetizes high-calibre people, you need to make decisions that scare them, in a good way. You need to choose paths that make them say, "They're going for it."

There's a reason the most transformative builders in any industry look a little unhinged at first. They closed doors that others wouldn't. They said no to backup plans. They invested in clarity over comfort. It wasn't because they were reckless; it was because they understood what obsession demands. It demands full weight. It requires choosing before you're selected. It demands that you let go of options to build something worth choosing at all.

When you cut optionality, you create pressure. But not the kind that crushes you, the kind that sharpens you. That pressure forces your best thinking. It kills laziness. It eliminates half-hearted execution. You can't afford to show up halfway when there's no exit. You build as if your future depends on it, because it does.

Eventually, you realize that the scariest thing is not being wrong. The most frightening thing is never knowing what you could have built if you'd just committed. That fear should not paralyze you. It should wake you up. It should push you to stop juggling and start building.

Obsession can't share its time. It wants all of you. And the moment you give it that, the options you left behind won't feel like sacrifices. They'll feel like clarifications. Like the shedding of everything that never really mattered.

Chapter 18: Conviction Without Consensus

Strategic obsession doesn't wait for a permission slip. It moves forward before the crowd claps. It operates on the unsettling but necessary principle that the right path often begins in isolation. Conviction is not validated by consensus; the absence of it tests it. And for anyone playing a long, high-stakes game, this is one of the earliest and most brutal lessons: if you need agreement to act, you'll never lead.

Consensus feels safe. It creates a shared illusion of correctness. If others agree, we must be on track. But consensus is slow. It lags behind the curve of innovation, creativity, and bold decision-making. It rewards the familiar, the proven, the already understood. Obsession doesn't operate in those conditions. Obsession lives in the edges, where certainty hasn't formed, where data is sparse, and where belief has to precede evidence.

Conviction, by contrast, is lonely. It means you've done the work others haven't. You've run deeper simulations. You've spent more time wrestling with the trade-offs. You've considered what could go wrong and still chosen to proceed. That kind of conviction doesn't shout. It doesn't require applause. It simply keeps moving. And because it does, it builds a different type of authority, one that is earned rather than granted.

The world confuses confidence with consensus because it's easier to outsource belief. If enough smart people say the same thing, it feels safer to align with them than to develop your thesis.

But obsession forces internal reckoning. It asks: Do I believe this enough to act before anyone else does? Do I care enough to look stupid for a while? Do I trust my process sufficiently to stand in silence while others doubt?

Most people don't. They hedge. They float in the safe zone of "we'll see." But obsession isn't neutral. It doesn't flirt with ideas. It weds them. And in doing so, it often becomes the outlier. That's the price. When your standard of proof is internal, not social, you make decisions others won't. You move when they're waiting. You bet on things they still don't understand. You are, for a time, misunderstood.

That misunderstanding is a crucible. It tests the depth of your belief. If your conviction depends on applause, you won't survive the silence. But if your sentence is earned, through repetition, thought, and immersion, it becomes unshakable. It becomes an engine. And over time, it becomes contagious. The very people who questioned you begin to mimic your clarity. They start citing your language. They look to your moves for direction.

But that comes later. First, you must withstand the void. Obsession gives you the stamina to persist through that void. It quiets the part of you that craves validation and sharpens the part that knows why you started. It keeps you building when the market ignores you. It keeps you refining when the audience misunderstands. It keeps you believing when the data is incomplete. Because obsession is not just passion, it's a decision repeated through friction.

Conviction without consensus also reveals who you are. You learn whether your strategy is performative or principled. You know if you're acting to be liked or acting to build. These are uncomfortable realizations. Most people conflate success with affirmation. But obsession doesn't care to be liked; it cares to be accurate, durable, and transformative. It's not reactive. It's directional.

That's why strategic obsession often comes across as arrogance, until it works. Then it's called vision. But the ingredients never changed. The same belief that initially seemed naive becomes genius in retrospect. Not because the world changed, but because results arrived. And once results arrive, consensus comes rushing in to claim they saw it all along. They didn't. They followed you because you moved without needing them to.

There is a line in the mind where consensus ends, and conviction begins. Most never cross it. They stop when their ideas make others uncomfortable. They shrink when faced with disapproval. But obsession demands you cross that line. Not recklessly. Not defiantly. But intentionally. That line marks the point where you leave behind the safety of the crowd and step into the risk of leadership.

Genuine innovation does not happen inside consensus. It occurs in the margins when someone refuses to lower their standard just to fit the room. Strategic obsession gives you the courage to hold the line. To protect the idea when it's fragile. To refine it in private until it can withstand public scrutiny. And to know, deep down, that the value of what you're building doesn't depend on how many people get it today.

Conviction doesn't mean never listening. It means listening with discernment. You're not ignoring the world. You're weighing it. You separate signal from noise. You differentiate helpful critique from emotional resistance. And you stay open to iteration, but not at the cost of dilution. You adapt where it sharpens, not where it softens.

Eventually, if you've built something worth building, consensus may find you. The market may catch up. The crowd may cheer. But by then, you won't need it. You will have already built the thing that proved your point. You will have already crossed the chasm. And you'll look back and realize consensus wasn't the goal. It was the echo.

Obsession doesn't wait for the echo. It speaks before the sound. It builds when there's no audience. It decides before the data. Because that's how the future gets made, not by those who ask for permission, but by those who act with conviction when the room is still full of doubt.

Chapter 19: Saying No to the Next Shiny Thing

The world doesn't lack opportunity. It lacks discernment. Every day, new tools emerge, new markets form, and the latest trends ignite. And every one of them comes wrapped in the same seductive pitch: "Don't miss this." It's a narrative designed to prey on your ambition, one that equates relevance with responsiveness. But for the strategically obsessed, saying yes to everything is the same as saying yes to nothing.

Obsession doesn't chase shiny things. It questions them. It interrogates the cost of distraction. Because when you're building something lasting, the scarcest resource is not money, not talent, not information, it's attention. Your attention is the currency of your progress. Every new interest you entertain demands a withdrawal from your primary mission. And those withdrawals add up, slowly, invisibly, until you're broke in all the ways that matter.

The shiny thing is never just a tool or idea. It's a temptation. It offers novelty when the work gets boring. It promises momentum when progress feels slow. It gives you an excuse to pivot, to start over, to feel like you're moving without actually enduring. And worst of all, it provides a socially acceptable way to abandon your path. After all, who could blame you for exploring a "hot new space"?

But obsession doesn't need novelty. It finds depth in repetition. It discovers new layers not by switching tracks but by going further into the one already chosen. The more you say no to shiny things, the more you refine your process. The more you uncover what others miss. The more you understand the hidden dynamics of your domain, the better you can navigate it. The more you can. This is not stubbornness. This is mastery.

The strategically obsessed understand that every "yes" has a shadow price. A new project doesn't just take time; it takes recovery. It takes switching costs. It fragments your mental model. Even when you try to juggle both, you're paying in quality, in consistency, in coherence. And what suffers most is not the new pursuit, it's the original one. The one that needed your full weight. The one that had compounding power. The one that might have become remarkable if only you had stayed.

To build something exceptional, you must become suspicious of easy excitement. You must learn to distrust anything that arrives fully packaged and universally praised. Because by the time something is shiny, it's already common. The opportunity has moved upstream, and you're left chasing echoes. The work that truly matters often feels boring in the middle. That boredom is not a signal to pivot; it's a test.

The shiny thing appears most seductive when you're in the valley of effort. When your current pursuit feels murky, when results are delayed, when the fun has faded into process. That's when distraction disguises itself as a new beginning. But what you're being offered is a reset, a fresh start with all the difficulty deferred. And resets, while tempting, are where potential goes to die.

The irony is that the longer you stay focused, the more your judgment improves. You begin to see through fads. You can tell the difference between a breakthrough and a gimmick. You stop mistaking urgency for opportunity. You ask better questions: Does this fit my thesis? Will this compound with what I've already built? Am I saying yes to this because it's right, or because I'm tired of the hard part?

When you build with obsession, the hard part isn't a signal to quit. It's where the real work begins. It's the part most people never reach because they've already been seduced by something shinier. This is why focused builders appear slow; they resist distraction longer than most. But that slowness is deceptive. Over time, it becomes speed. Because what they're building is coherent. Aligned. Cumulative.

The cost of saying yes to the wrong thing is rarely visible in the moment. It shows up later, in missed breakthroughs, fractured brand identities, diluted energy, and the slow erosion of trust in yourself. Each shiny detour sends a message to your subconscious: I don't believe this is going to work. I don't trust myself to endure. And eventually, that message embeds itself so deeply that commitment starts to feel unnatural.

To avoid this, the obsessed create guardrails. They pre-decide what they will and won't entertain. They don't evaluate every new thing on the fly. They define filters based on mission, values, and momentum. If an opportunity doesn't amplify what's already working, it's ignored, no matter how tempting it looks. This kind of discipline feels rigid to outsiders. But it's what protects the builder from self-sabotage.

This doesn't mean you reject all innovation. It means you evaluate it through the lens of your mission. You don't bolt on every new feature; you ask whether it aligns with your strategic core. You don't chase every trend; you ask whether it fits your long-term positioning. You treat new tools as optional, not essential. And when you do adopt something new, it's not out of FOMO. It's out of fit.

There's freedom in this. When you stop chasing the shiny thing, you regain control over your time, your thinking, and your identity. You no longer wake up wondering what to pursue; you already know. You move deeper, not wider. And in doing so, you build something others can't imitate. Something grounded. Something real.

The world rewards novelty in the short term. But over time, it's depth that wins. And depth only emerges when you say no to everything that tries to lure you away from it. The shiny thing will always be there. But so will the mission, waiting for you to choose it again.

Chapter 20: Don't Compete. Out-Commit.

In any crowded market, the first instinct is to compete. Compete on price. Compete on features. Compete on marketing tactics, positioning, distribution, and speed. You try to be better, louder, faster, brighter. You measure yourself against the benchmark and obsess over closing the gap. But obsession doesn't look sideways. It doesn't spend its time in comparison. It operates in a different dimension. It doesn't try to outshine, it out-commits.

The ones who win aren't always the most talented. They're often the ones who stayed when others left. Who got back up when others bowed out. Who kept showing up after the applause stopped. Competition creates tension. Commitment creates gravity. The market respects gravity. Customers feel it. Teams are stabilized by it. Momentum gathers around it. And it cannot be faked.

The builder driven by obsession doesn't scan the horizon for the next trend. They don't race to copy best practices. They sink into their conviction and commit deeper. This doesn't mean they're blind to the world; it means they see the world as noise until it aligns with their signal. They're not trying to take market share; they're building markets that others later regret ignoring.

To out-commit means to show up consistently long after others have lost interest. It means tedious repetitions of excellence. It means saying no to shortcuts that could produce a bump today but damage trust tomorrow. It means holding yourself to a standard that no one is watching, yet. You're not competing for attention. You're building for inevitability.

The dangerous thing about competition is that it subtly shifts your goals. You begin to measure progress by proximity to others, not proximity to your mission. Your metrics start to reflect movement, not meaning. And soon you find yourself optimizing for optics rather than substance. You look successful on paper, but hollow on the inside. Commitment recalibrates that. It puts your eyes back where they belong, on the work, not the race.

Obsession sharpens this even further. It makes you immune to applause. Not ungrateful, but unmoved. You don't need praise to push forward. You don't need headlines to keep shipping. You move because you have to. Because the mission demands it. Because the idea hasn't finished speaking yet. You build when no one is watching. You refine when no one is asking. You persist when no one believes. And then, when the results arrive, they look inevitable. But only because you made them so.

Out-committing doesn't just apply to time; it applies to depth. You go further into the problem than anyone else. You know the nuances they've overlooked. You see the patterns they miss. You listen to customers more closely. You take feedback more seriously. You document what others gloss over. Your product feels different, not because it looks flashier, but because it's built with more care. Because it's grounded in more context. Because it reflects a more profound willingness to stay in the room until it's right.

This is how you become incomparable. When you stop playing by the rules of the category, you stop being measured by them. You're no longer in the running for "best" in a narrow race;

you're defining a new terrain altogether. And that terrain is built on obsession. On depth. On devotion. Competitors might still appear on the radar, but they're not building what you're building. They're not willing to suffer what you've endured. And that difference creates separation, permanent separation.

There's a reason the most iconic creators, companies, and leaders seem both familiar and untouchable. It's not because they were chosen. It's because they decided for themselves. Again. And again. And again. They didn't just get lucky. They got durable. And that durability came from an obsession that refused to dilute, and a commitment that refused to end early.

There will always be someone with more reach, more money, more polish. That's fine. Let them have it. While they advertise, you iterate. While they scale, you improve. While they posture, you practice. And while they play games of optics, you build something that quietly becomes the benchmark. Not because you competed harder. Because you committed deeper.

This approach is not glamorous. It's gritty. It's invisible. It's late nights without recognition. It's long stretches without feedback. It's seasons where the only person who believes is you. And it's precisely what separates the remembered from the forgotten. The ones who go all in, even when it doesn't make sense to anyone else, are the ones who bend reality over time.

This kind of commitment isn't just professional. It's personal. It shows up in how you lead, how you listen, and how you make decisions under pressure. It shows up in the culture you build, the contracts you sign, and the promises you keep. Commitment, in the hands of the obsessed, becomes contagious. It attracts people who want to go deep, not just go fast. And with the right people, depth becomes unstoppable.

Don't compete. Out-commit. Out-commit your former self. Out-commit your former ceiling. Out-commit the expectations others placed on you. Let the competitors run their race. Let them win their rounds. You're not here for the trophy. You're here for the truth. And truth is built by those who stay.

Chapter 21: When Others Get Distracted

Distraction is the silent killer of potential. It doesn't announce itself with urgency or violence. It just whispers, endlessly, pulling your focus a fraction of a degree off-centre until one day, your work is no longer yours. It's reactive. It's scattered. It's guided by trend cycles, comparison, commentary, and anything but clarity. This is how most people lose. Not because they weren't talented. Not because they didn't care. But because they didn't protect their focus long enough for it to harden into something formidable.

The strategically obsessed don't just resist distraction. They weaponize its absence. They understand that in a world that runs on short-term memory and dopamine loops, focus itself becomes a competitive advantage. When everyone else is pivoting, chasing, and reshuffling, you become lethal by staying rooted. Obsession doesn't ask for attention management hacks. It demands a lifestyle engineered for isolation from noise. It doesn't require you to do more; it requires you to be unavailable to anything that isn't the mission.

Distraction thrives on external urgency. It arrives disguised as opportunity, as obligation, as relevance. An email, a new platform, a competitor's pivot, a market shift. These things demand a response, but obsession trains you to ask: Does this require my response? Is this a disruption or data? Am I reacting or recommitting? When you default to recommitment instead of reaction, you become impossible to destabilize.

This is where you become dangerous. When others can be lured away with shiny objects, you go silent and build. When their energy splinters into dozens of conversations, you disappear into deep work. And when they surface, needing validation or adjustment, you're already on the other side of the problem, with leverage they didn't see forming. Not because you were better. But because you stayed.

Obsession isn't about avoiding everything; it's about defending something. The mission becomes a fortress. Every yes is a gate left open, every distraction a point of entry for mediocrity. You start building your days, your habits, your boundaries around one question: Will this move the mission? If not, it's discarded without guilt. You don't argue with distractions. You starve them.

Over time, this refusal to be distracted compounds. Your work becomes more refined. Your instincts are sharper. Your ideas are more precise. While others are switching tools, you're mastering yours. While they're changing positioning, you're deepening your message. While they're building new things, you're building deeper roots into the thing that matters. And eventually, the weight of that focus becomes undeniable.

The most dangerous people in any space are not those with the best ideas. They're the ones who keep showing up to the same idea until it's undeniable. They make their work heavier with every iteration. They don't seek novelty to solve problems; they extract originality from commitment. They don't chase flow. They create a structure that makes deep work inevitable.

Distraction also erodes confidence. Each pivot weakens your sense of authority. Each shift away from your core adds noise to your intuition. You begin to outsource decisions to the market, to competitors, to advisors. Your voice fades under the volume of consensus. But obsession brings it back. It reconnects you with the thing only you can see. It restores your internal compass.

That doesn't mean ignoring the world. It means observing without orbiting. You study the signals without becoming reactive to them. You use the market as context, not as your North Star. Obsession lets you outlast volatility because you're not navigating by headlines. You're navigating by principles. And principles don't shift with sentiment.

There's an eerie calm that comes over the obsessed. Not because they're relaxed, but because they're anchored. While others scramble for visibility, they pursue precision. While others debate tactics, they hone execution. While others focus on performance metrics, they prioritize depth. And in the long run, depth is undefeated.

You become dangerous because you become invisible to the algorithm of distraction. The same systems that keep others spinning, notifications, feedback loops, and social noise, don't touch you. Not because you're immune, but because you've opted out. You've designed your life to protect your edge. And you've made peace with being misunderstood while you refine it.

This level of focus is not standard because it is not easy. It demands trade-offs. It demands saying no when yes would be more flattering. It requires walking away from good things to preserve great things. It demands boredom. Stillness. Repetition. But these are not signs of decay, they're signs of depth. And depth, once acquired, makes you immovable.

Your danger doesn't come from aggression. It comes from consistency. From discipline. From the compounding returns of doing the right thing longer than anyone else was willing to. Distraction fractures effort. But obsession creates gravity. And gravity pulls everything else toward it: opportunity, talent, capital, attention. Not because you shouted. Because you stayed.

When others get distracted, you don't just avoid it. You use it. You let their flinch create your window. You let their attention loss become your leverage gain. You let their noise amplify your silence. Because silence, in the hands of the obsessed, is not emptiness. It's momentum. Waiting. Pressurizing. Preparing to strike with a force that can't be matched by someone who's only half present.

Let others chase the next thing. You'll build the next standard.

Chapter 22: Obsession Is a Risk Multiplier

Risk is often misunderstood. It's painted as recklessness, as the decision to leap without looking, as the currency of gamblers and outliers. But in truth, risk is not the act of leaping; it's the condition of living. Every decision you make is a bet. Every direction you take closes off others. The question is not whether you're taking risks. It's whether you're doing it with awareness, intention, and strategy.

Obsession doesn't eliminate risk. It amplifies it. And that's what makes it powerful.

When you pursue something with your full weight, you raise the stakes. You concentrate your bets. You become emotionally, financially, and reputationally exposed. You remove the safety nets. And in doing so, you create the pressure required to generate extraordinary results. This is why most people avoid obsession. It doesn't feel safe. It doesn't allow you to hedge. But if you want uncommon returns, you must accept uncommon exposure.

Most people seek to mitigate risk by diversifying their attention. They split focus across multiple pursuits. They keep fallback plans warm. They refuse to commit in case the first thing doesn't work. And in doing so, they limit their upside. Obsession says: go all in. Not unthinkingly. Not carelessly. But fully. Because no serious breakthrough has ever been achieved by someone half-invested.

Obsession multiplies risk by collapsing your identity into your mission. You're no longer just doing a job. You're making a declaration. This is who I am. This is what I built. This is what I stand for. That identification raises the cost of failure, but it also unlocks levels of clarity and force that no casual player can access. When your name is on the line, you move differently. You become intolerant of mediocrity. You start measuring progress by personal standards, not industry ones.

There's a paradox here. Obsession multiplies risk, but it also multiplies your ability to manage it. Because obsession brings awareness, it heightens your pattern recognition. It makes you more sensitive to threats, more responsive to shifts, and more committed to preparation. The person with scattered focus tends to take uncalculated risks. The obsessed builder takes informed, deliberate dangers because they're closer to the ground. They're not reacting to the headlines; they're embedded in the terrain.

Strategic obsession is not about blind sacrifice. It's about concentrated strategy. You're not saying "yes" to everything. You're saying "yes" to the few things that matter most, and "no" to everything else. That kind of narrowing is what raises the stakes. But it's also what increases the probability of success. You're not diluted. You're aligned. And aligned energy consistently outperforms scattered intent.

There's also the risk of being misunderstood. Obsession will make your decisions look irrational to others. You'll be told to slow down, to hedge, to be realistic. But realism is often a disguise for fear. And obsession cannot be governed by fear. It must be governed by principle, by vision, and by endurance. If you let fear set your limits, you've already lost the most essential advantage obsession gives you: momentum.

Momentum, once it compounds, can reduce your risk. You gain leverage. You gain allies. You gain data. You create self-reinforcing systems that stabilize your trajectory. But none of that begins without risk at the front. You must walk through the uncertainty. You must stake your reputation before it's too late. You must say, "I believe this is worth it," without needing consensus or proof.

This is not a call to recklessness. Strategic obsession calculates risk through a different lens. It doesn't ask, "What's the worst that could happen?" It asks, "What's the cost of never going all in?" The cost of wasted time, potential, and diluted purpose is far more dangerous than short-term failure. The obsessed don't fear loss. They fear regret.

And so they lean in. They take asymmetric bets. They double down on their thesis. They invest in ideas others still dismiss as fringe. They choose depth over breadth, quality over convenience, precision over speed. They accept that they may fail louder, but also that they will succeed deeper. Because obsession doesn't just multiply risk, it multiplies meaning.

The relationship between risk and meaning is often ignored. We pretend we can live safe lives and still feel fulfilled. But it doesn't work that way. Fulfillment comes from friction. From daring to want something so badly that your failure would hurt. From caring enough to try when there are easier paths available. Obsession doesn't shield you from that; it demands it. And in return, it offers a kind of clarity you can't buy or fake.

You become the kind of person who lives in alignment with what you value most, not occasionally, but perpetually. The type of person who builds, not because it's profitable, but because it's necessary. The kind of person who isn't trying to escape risk, but to master it.

In the end, obsession is the ultimate risk amplifier, not because it leads to chaos, but because it insists on coherence. It forces you to unify your actions, your identity, and your direction. That unification exposes you, but it also empowers you. Because once you're fully in, you're playing a different game. You're not betting pieces of your energy across many tables. You're pushing every chip forward because you finally believe the work is worth it.

And that belief, that ferocious, disciplined belief, is what separates the forgettable from the indelible. Obsession may multiply your risk, but it also multiplies your odds of mattering.

Chapter 23: What You Sustain, Sustains You

Obsession isn't a surge. It's a rhythm. A long arc of commitment that outlives the noise and settles into something elemental. In the beginning, you push the work. You initiate, you sacrifice, you stretch. But eventually, if the foundation is proper, something changes: the work begins to go back. It starts to give more than it takes. It starts to sustain you.

That's the inflection point strategic obsession aims for, not just success, not just notoriety, but self-reinforcing contribution. You build something that feeds you, not just financially, but emotionally, mentally, and even spiritually. But that state doesn't arrive quickly. It is earned through sustained effort, consistent refinement, and a relationship with the work that transcends mood.

We live in a world obsessed with launches of products, books, startups, and movements. But obsession is not defined by how you start. It's characterized by how long you can hold the tension. Most people start strong but often burn out. Their energy was real, but it wasn't renewable. It was hype-powered, not purpose-powered. And when the buzz faded, so did they.

Sustainability is not a compromise. It's a strategy. It means building in a way that allows for endurance, consistency, and depth. The obsessed don't burn bright and disappear. They burn steadily and transform. They treat the work like a system, not a sprint. They design their schedules, teams, and priorities around staying power. They optimize for longevity, not just velocity.

What you sustain, sustains you. When you return to the same idea, day after day, with care and rigour, it begins to evolve with you. It becomes richer, more nuanced. You no longer need to reinvent yourself every quarter; you refine. You no longer look for new distractions; you deepen your craft. That deepening becomes its reward. It energizes you because it reveals parts of yourself you didn't know existed.

The most significant misstep ambitious people make is confusing friction with misalignment. The moment things get difficult, they pivot. But obsession reframes friction. It says, "Good. Now we're in the part that matters." It sees difficulty not as a sign to quit, but as proof that the work is beginning to shape you. And when you let the work shape you, when you stay long enough for it to challenge your assumptions, you start to change in ways that outlast the project itself.

This is the quiet truth of obsession: it is reciprocal. You shape the work, but the work shapes you. Your discipline becomes devotion. Your attention becomes precision. Your doubts become fuel. And eventually, the act of sustaining becomes the source of your edge. While others are stuck in cycles of starting over, you are reaping the compound interest of staying in.

Sustainability isn't just about avoiding burnout; it's about building rhythm. Ritual. Architecture. You don't sprint until you collapse. You build processes that protect your energy. You create systems that let you go deeper without drowning. You stop chasing flow and start making it, daily, with or without inspiration. Because real flow doesn't come from novelty, it comes from intimacy with your craft.

Over time, this creates identity-level change. You stop seeing yourself as someone trying to accomplish something and start seeing yourself as someone who is simply living out their design. The effort becomes integrated. It's not a job anymore. It's not even a mission. It's you. And because it's you, it's sustainable. What you sustain, sustains you.

This is why the obsessed protect their process so fiercely. They are not just safeguarding output; they are protecting the internal ecosystem that allows obsession to thrive. They know that small daily disciplines, if honoured over time, become unbreakable scaffolding for greatness. That even the act of returning, of showing up when it's hard, is a source of power.

Eventually, people begin to notice, not because you shouted, but because you endured. Not because you went viral, but because you were still here. Still building and still improving. And that endurance becomes trust not just with the market, but with yourself. You begin to trust your capacity. You stop fearing the complex parts. You start seeking them because you know that beyond each one is a new version of you.

This trust is not loud. It doesn't need affirmation. It doesn't need to be advertised. It manifests in how you walk, how you decide, and how you build. People feel it. It anchors teams. It calms volatility. It makes the impossible seem manageable because you're not relying on inspiration to keep going. You're relying on rhythm.

Strategic obsession, when sustained, creates quiet power. The kind that doesn't blink when others panic. The kind that doesn't dilute when others chase trends. The kind that, over time, becomes magnetic. You stop chasing opportunity, and opportunity starts chasing you, not because of luck, but because you've become a reliable signal in a chaotic world.

Most people never reach this state. They think the goal is to finish. But obsession knows the goal is to continue. To refine. To persist. To sustain. And in that commitment, the work stops being a burden. It becomes a source. Of clarity. Of momentum. Of meaning.

In the end, what you sustain, sustains you. The real reward of obsession is not just what you build, but what it creates in you.

Chapter 24: The Final Inch

It's not the first ninety-nine percent that breaks most people. It's the last inch. The moment where momentum fades, where results stall, where fatigue peaks, and doubt reappears with sharper teeth. At that edge, most relent. They rationalize, reframe, retreat. They say, "It's good enough," or "It's not worth it," or "No one will notice." And maybe no one would. But obsession notices. Obsession demands the final inch.

The final inch isn't glamorous. It doesn't come with applause or even acknowledgment. It's the part no one else sees, the second draft of the third version, the late-night bug fix, the choice to keep tightening when everyone else has already let go. And that's what makes it sacred. Because the final inch is where quality lives, it's where mastery separates itself from competence. It's where the work crosses over from good to unmistakable.

This is the part of the game that obsession was built for. Strategic obsession doesn't just give you a strong start. It provides you with finishing power. It gives you the precision to notice when something is 99% right, and the discipline to keep going anyway. It gives you the resilience to push when the emotional rewards are gone. Because the final inch is not driven by excitement, standards drive it.

High standards are what make the final inch visible in the first place. Most people don't realize they're close to greatness; they stop when they get tired. The obsessed stop when it's right. And they know it's right not because someone else approved it, but because it meets the private criteria no one else even knows exists. That internal calibration is the engine of excellence.

The world is full of almost-finished greatness. Books abandoned in final edits. Startups that shipped too soon. Relationships that broke because the complicated conversation never happened. Products that were ninety percent there but never earned loyalty because the last ten percent was where trust lived. And the ten percent? It's made up of inches. Final inches.

You earn those inches through persistence, but you claim them through patience. Strategic obsession gives you both. It gives you the tunnel vision to keep showing up and the wide-angle lens to remember why it matters. Without obsession, you don't make it to the final inch. You talk yourself out of it. You call it a distraction or diminishing returns. You convince yourself that you could be using your time elsewhere. But obsession doesn't let you move on. It pulls you back. One more hour. One more draft. One more pass.

Sometimes, the final inch is not even functional. It's aesthetic. It's emotional. It's about feeling. The way the sentence lands. The way the colour aligns with the tone. The way the strategy not only works but resonates. These are the details that data can't always catch, but that obsession can. Because obsession doesn't just care about the outcome, it cares about fidelity. About integrity. About wholeness.

And yes, the final inch often looks excessive to outsiders. People will say, "No one will notice that." And most won't. But the right people will. The right partners. The right customers. The right collaborators. The ones who are playing a long game themselves. And they'll see it for what it is: a signal. A mark that you care enough to do what didn't need to be done. A declaration that your standard isn't dependent on surveillance.

What obsession understands is that greatness compounds at the edges. That while 80% of success might come from fundamentals, the final 20%, the part that people remember, that gets talked about, that sets you apart, is made of the inches others left on the table. Most people are good with good enough. You are not most people. Obsession makes sure of that.

It also rewires your relationship with fatigue. When others are worn out, obsession turns fatigue into focus. The tiredness doesn't make you sloppy; it makes you sharper. More deliberate. More selective. Because when your energy is low, only the essentials remain. And when you're obsessed, the essentials are obvious. They point you toward the final inch.

The final inch is where obsession becomes visible. It's the difference between a presentation and a message. Between a launch and a legacy. Between something that ships and something that lasts. You don't get there by accident. You get there by refusing to leave early, by choosing to end strong.

The truth is, no one knows what your final inch is but you. No one knows what was left unsaid, what was nearly fixed, what you saw but chose to ignore. And no one will know if you pushed through, except you. That's why obsession is required. Not because others will applaud it, but because you will carry it.

This is the weight the obsessed carry with pride: the knowledge that they went all the way. That they honoured the work. That they finished what they started and then finished it again. Because the final inch isn't about perfection, it's about completeness. And completeness doesn't mean polished. It means true. Finished not just in appearance, but in essence.

And when you cross that inch, you don't just ship a better product. You become a better builder. A clearer thinker. A more dangerous competitor. Because you've proven, again, that your standards can survive fatigue, pressure, and time, that's what makes the final inch so powerful. It's not what you gain from crossing it. It's who you become for having done it.

Chapter 25: Borrowed Time, Owned Outcomes

Most people move like they have time to spare. They schedule their ambitions between meetings, defer the hard decisions until things "settle down," and keep their most important work as a someday project, tucked behind urgent noise. But obsession doesn't wait for someday. It operates with the constant awareness that time is not promised, it's borrowed—and borrowed time demands owned outcomes.

When you act like time is borrowed, you stop assuming the future will hold space for your priorities. You often delay your most meaningful work until next quarter, the following hire, or the next break in the calendar. You realize that the distance between "wanting" and "doing" is the difference between building something that matters and dying with good ideas.

This is the mindset that obsession enforces. It doesn't allow for drift. It doesn't respect indecision. It doesn't romanticize potential. It demands movement now. Because now is all you have guaranteed. Not in theory, but in fact. And while others hesitate, calibrate, and wait for perfect clarity, you move. Not recklessly, but urgently. With intent. With reverence for the window of time you're occupying.

There's a discipline that emerges when you truly internalize borrowed time. You stop measuring effort in hours and start measuring it in integrity. Did I give today what the mission deserved? Did I put enough weight behind the things that matter

most? Did I choose the hard thing over the convenient one?
These are not efficiency questions. They're ownership questions.

Strategic obsession takes those questions and builds a rhythm
around them. It stops asking for permission to prioritize what
matters. It clears the table and makes space for the real work. It
doesn't seek balance. It seeks alignment. Because when your
actions reflect your values, you stop wasting time on narratives
that no longer serve you.

But most people don't operate this way. They move like they
have a bottomless runway. They treat their days like drafts. They
assume there will be another chance to say what needs saying, to
ship what needs building, to repair what needs fixing. But
obsession strips away that illusion. It forces you to see the
opportunity cost of your delays. Not in dollars, but in direction. In
momentum. In identity.

The hard truth is that every day you defer your real work is a
day your edge dulls. Not just because others might move faster,
but because your conviction fades in the presence of inaction.
Action reinforces belief. Inaction erodes it. You can't stay
obsessed with something you don't touch. Obsession requires
engagement. Daily. Intentionally. Relentlessly.

This doesn't mean working nonstop. It means living
deliberately. It means choosing how you show up, where you put
your focus, and what you're willing to abandon so your mission
can breathe. Most people say yes to too much because they're
afraid of being rude. The obsessed say no because they're so
scared of being average.

And they understand that borrowed time comes with
accountability. If you have only a limited number of hours, days,

or cycles, then what you choose to build becomes your signature. There is no one else to blame. No institution, algorithm, or team to hide behind. This is your life. Your path. Your outcomes. Own them.

Ownership is not about control. It's about acceptance. It's the decision to be the architect of your time, not the tenant of someone else's priorities. That means confronting your distractions and naming your avoidance strategies. And being brutally honest about the ways you've misused the time you were given. Not to wallow, but to redirect. Quickly. Decisively.

The best builders, the most obsessed creators, all carry this weight. They know the clock is ticking. They see the opportunity as fragile. And instead of panicking, they focus. They collapse their attention into the task at hand. Not because it's trendy, but because it's theirs. Because they've decided that if time is borrowed, then today will not be wasted.

This urgency is not frantic. It's composed. It's quiet. It's structured. It shows up in how you write your emails, how you take your meetings, and how you cut features that don't matter. It shows up in how you cancel obligations that drain you. In how you protect your calendar like it's your operating system, because it is.

Borrowed time creates boundaries. It makes it easier to say no, not because you're too busy, but because you're too clear. And that clarity becomes contagious. Teams that see leaders operating with that kind of urgency begin to calibrate differently. They stop asking "how fast can we move?" and start asking "how aligned can we be?", which is where real speed begins.

The irony of acting on borrowed time is that it often leads to more time. The faster you eliminate friction, the more margin you create. The more decisively you move, the fewer decisions you have to revisit. The more consistently you deliver, the more momentum you gain. And momentum, once compounded, begins to buy you time in ways the distracted can't imagine.

But none of this happens by default. The default is drift. The default is busy but misaligned. The default is urgent but unanchored. Obsession rewrites that default. It says: This matters. This is mine. And I will not treat it like an afterthought.

In the end, the question isn't "how much time do I have?" The question is "what will I do with the time I've already been given?" If the answer is anything less than full ownership, then don't be surprised when your outcomes reflect hesitation instead of commitment.

You don't get to choose how much time you have. But you do get to choose what you build with it. Make it count.

Chapter 26: The Obsession Feedback Loop

Obsession is not a fixed trait. It's a system. A living, adaptive loop that strengthens with use and weakens with neglect. Most people think obsession is something you either have or don't, an innate drive, a personality quirk, a streak of intensity that shows up in certain types. But obsession, at its core, is built. Reinforced. Sustained. And the mechanism that creates it is the feedback loop.

Every action you take toward your mission is either feeding that loop or starving it. Obsession doesn't grow from intensity alone. It grows from reinforcement. You take an action. That action produces evidence. That evidence fuels belief. And belief drives the following action, often with more clarity, more precision, more speed. Over time, that cycle becomes self-reinforcing. You're no longer chasing motivation. You're operating from momentum.

This is the difference between the casually ambitious and the strategically obsessed. The casually ambitious wait for validation before they commit. They dip in and out, responding to energy spikes, external praise, or bursts of enthusiasm. The obsessed don't wait for the loop to form. They create it manually. They act first. They give the system something to build from. And once the loop catches, it does the rest.

But it has to be protected.

The obsession loop is fragile at first. It needs repetition, not results. In the early stages, the outcomes might be small, even invisible. But if the effort is consistent, a pattern begins to form. You start to see signals. You notice friction decreasing, resonance increasing. You see the rough shape of the future you're building. And that signal, even faint, is enough to keep going—enough to turn attention into allegiance.

Every time you act in alignment with your mission, you strengthen the loop. Every time you compromise, defer, or dilute your focus, you weaken it. That's why the obsessed are so ruthless with their attention. They're not just trying to get things done; they're maintaining the integrity of the system that powers their progress. The loop is sacred. And when it breaks, they feel it immediately.

Sustaining the loop requires more than output. It requires feedback. But not all feedback is equal. The obsessed are selective. They don't outsource belief to external applause. They don't need trending metrics or likes to know they're on the right path. Instead, they look for high-quality signals: the tightness of their ideas, the clarity of their decision-making, the internal sense that things are compounding.

That internal signal is the most powerful form of feedback. It doesn't fluctuate with the market. It doesn't depend on noise. It's calibrated to your progress. But it only becomes accurate when you're in motion. Action is the calibration mechanism. The more you build, the more honest your internal signal becomes. And the more truthful it is, the more confidently you can act. The loop tightens.

What the outside world calls "vision" is often just a highly tuned feedback loop. You move, you observe, you refine. You don't need to predict the future; you need to interpret your system. That's how strategic obsession avoids the trap of fantasy. It's grounded. It doesn't just dream, it tracks, adjusts, and sharpens in real time.

But beware: the loop can turn against you. Just as positive actions create upward momentum, negative actions create decay. One missed day becomes two. One compromise opens the door to rationalization. Deciding for comfort instead of alignment erodes trust in your system. And suddenly, the loop is spinning, but in reverse.

This is why strategic obsession is so often mistaken for extremism. It looks intense. It looks severe. But what it is… is protective. The obsessed know how easy it is to lose the thread. So, they build routines, structures, and rituals that keep the loop intact. They remove decision fatigue. They automate the beginnings of their days. They create environments that make the right choice automatic.

They understand that discipline is not the opposite of freedom; it's the engine of it. Because when the loop is strong, you don't need to negotiate with yourself. You don't need to hype yourself into action. You don't even need to feel inspired. You move. And every movement adds another rotation to the wheel.

Over time, the loop becomes culture. It's not just how you operate, it's how your team operates. Everyone understands the rhythm. Everyone feels the compounding. And when something breaks the loop, a distraction, a project that doesn't align, a shift in direction, everyone notices. Because when obsession is embedded at the core, dilution is not just inefficient. It's intolerable.

And here's the secret: once the loop is mature, it generates energy. The same way a flywheel gains momentum with each spin, your obsession loop becomes a source of power. You wake up clearer. You execute faster. You recover from setbacks with more clarity. You don't need to be told what to do, you know, because the loop is talking back to you.

This is where obsession transcends motivation. You are no longer relying on mood. You are no longer waiting to feel like it. You're executing from identity, from infrastructure, from momentum. And that kind of motion is hard to stop. Not because it's loud. But because it's self-sustaining.

To the outside world, it might look like you're relentless. But inside the loop, it feels peaceful. Steady. Grounded. Because you're no longer negotiating with distraction. You're no longer entertaining alternatives. You've chosen. You've committed. And now, the loop does what it was designed to do: it reinforces what you've decided matters most.

In the end, obsession isn't a fire you have to keep lighting. It's a loop you have to keep feeding. Feed it well, and it will feed you back tenfold.

Chapter 27: Your Identity Is the Infrastructure

At some point in every long-term pursuit, strategy alone stops being enough. You can have the right frameworks, the right goals, the right timing, but still find yourself stuck, resisting your progress. Why? Because the infrastructure of obsession isn't just external. It's internal. It's not only about what you do. It's about who you believe you are.

Your identity is the infrastructure. It holds the weight of your actions. It determines what behaviours feel natural, what sacrifices feel reasonable, and what commitments feel aligned. And if your identity is misaligned with your mission, you'll sabotage your progress, quietly, repeatedly, unconsciously.

This is why obsession isn't just a pattern of behaviour. It's a shift in self-perception. It's the decision to become the kind of person who stays, who sharpens, who pushes, who finishes. Without that internal shift, every external strategy will eventually falter. You'll revert to who you believe yourself to be, not who you say you want to become.

Most people never interrogate the infrastructure of their identity. They build goals on top of old patterns. They stack new behaviours on top of outdated narratives. They declare ambition, but their internal operating system still sees them as someone who quits early, doubts often, or settles for "good enough." The obsessed don't let that stand. They challenge it. They rewire it. They reconstruct themselves from the inside out.

You don't become someone obsessed with mastery by accident. You do it by deliberately choosing beliefs that support the weight of your ambition. Beliefs like: "I finish what I start." "I can do hard things." "I don't need to be the best; I need to be consistent." These aren't affirmations. They're anchor points. Identity statements that guide behaviour when motivation runs dry.

And once these beliefs are installed, action becomes easier. You stop white knuckling your way through resistance. You stop negotiating with distractions. You move because your identity demands it. Because it would be incongruent not to. Because it would feel unnatural to drift.

This is why behaviour change often fails in the absence of identity change. You try to build new habits without becoming someone who owns them. You try to practice consistency, but you don't believe you're capable of it. And the moment stress or ambiguity appears, you collapse back into old patterns, because that's what your identity has been rehearsing for years.

Obsession short-circuits this by making the mission personal. It fuses the work with the self. Not in an unhealthy, ego-driven way, but in a clear, aligned, responsibility-based way. "If I don't do this, it doesn't get done." That's not pressure. That's power. It's a declaration that you are the backbone of your trajectory. No one's coming to reinforce it for you.

This level of identity ownership doesn't happen overnight. It's sculpted. Brick by brick. Decision by decision. You start by acting as if you already are the person you want to become. You don't wait for confidence. You don't wait for proof. You build the identity through repetition. Through integrity. Through following through on your word.

Every time you keep a promise to yourself, you pour concrete into your foundation. Every time you abandon one, you introduce cracks. And over time, those cracks become your default. That's why the obsessed are so militant about their standards, not because they're perfectionists, but because they understand the cost of erosion.

Your identity is infrastructure. And like any infrastructure, it needs maintenance. Reflection. Repair. You must regularly audit your beliefs: Are they serving your mission? Are they rooted in clarity or fear? Are they making your standards feel inevitable or aspirational?

The obsessed ask these questions often. They catch identity drift before it derails momentum. They recalibrate when stress tempts them into old patterns. They recognize that their thoughts are not facts, but they are blueprints. And every blueprint either supports the mission or undermines it.

One of the most powerful upgrades you can make in a life of obsession is this: stop treating your beliefs as observations and start treating them as tools. You don't need to believe everything you think. You need to consider what helps you build. That doesn't mean delusion. It means design. Intentional mental architecture that reinforces your commitment instead of poking holes in it.

And yes, this takes effort. Identity work is slow. It's uncomfortable. It means letting go of old labels, outdated metrics, and the stories you've used to excuse your limits. It means rewriting your relationship with discomfort, failure, and even success. But on the other side of that effort is something rare: internal infrastructure that doesn't crack under pressure.

Once this is built, everything changes. You start moving faster, not because you're rushing, but because there's no more internal resistance. You stop second-guessing your path. You stop looking for external permission. You trust yourself because you've built self-worth. And the deeper that trust goes, the more freedom you gain.

Freedom not from discipline, but within it. Freedom to focus, to go deep, to say no without guilt. Freedom to build without applause. Because the applause doesn't shape you anymore, the work does. You've stopped outsourcing identity and started engineering it.

And now, your mission has a foundation it can stand on. Your goals have a home. Your decisions are clear. And your obsession has room to grow, no longer stifled by old stories, but supported by an identity that says: I do this. This is who I am. And this is what I finished.

Chapter 28: The Second Obsession

The first obsession builds you. It tears through your assumptions, sharpens your discipline, stretches your identity, and anchors your focus. It becomes the proving ground, the project, mission, or pursuit that forces you to become someone new. But eventually, you finish. You launch. You exit. You win. And then comes the quiet question: what now?

This is where many fall apart. They built everything around the intensity of that first chase. They rode the momentum, made the sacrifices, lived inside the obsession like it was a permanent state. But once it's done, they realize something uncomfortable: they never built a system for what comes next. They built a life for the fire, but not the aftermath. That's where the second obsession begins.

The second obsession is not just a new project. It's a test of sustainability. Of maturity. Of principle. The first one was about proof: Can I do this? The second one is about integration: Who am I now that I've done it? Can I sustain this level of focus without adrenaline? Can I commit again without novelty? Can I go deep without the pressure of a debut?

Most don't. They try to recreate the conditions of their first rise. They look for another high, another challenge, another identity to wrap themselves in. But the second obsession doesn't respond to hype. It doesn't bloom in chaos. It asks something more complicated: consistency without urgency. Devotion without the existential thrill. Refinement instead of reinvention.

And for many, that's terrifying. Because the second obsession is quieter, it doesn't announce itself. It waits for you to choose it, not as a saviour, but as a strategy. It forces you to ask, not what's next, but what's worth sustaining. It pushes you to shift from proving yourself to building something permanent. And in that shift, the game changes.

You begin to realize that obsession isn't just about ambition. It's about design. The first time, it was raw. Intuitive. Chaotic. You moved on instinct. You figured it out as you went. But now, you know better. You know how to set conditions. How to build scaffolding around your energy. How to protect your edge. You don't need to chase. You need to choose.

The second obsession is where strategic obsession truly earns its name. You're not reacting anymore. You're orchestrating. You're not just working hard, you're working precisely. The margin for error shrinks, but so does the noise. You become less interested in proving you're capable and more interested in establishing that your systems are.

This is the point at which obsession becomes legacy. Not because you're chasing recognition, but because you're building something that will survive your moods, your seasons, even your eventual exit. The second obsession forces long-term thinking, not in theory, but in architecture. You ask more complex questions: Will this scale? Will this evolve with me? Is this designed for depth or speed?

You also become a different kind of dangerous. Not because you're louder, but because you're quieter. You're less reactive. Less visible. But more grounded, more lethal in execution. You don't need attention to know you're doing it right. You're no longer chasing proof, you're compounding mastery.

There's also a humility that comes with the second obsession. You've seen what it costs. You've lived through the trade-offs, the tension, the near-burnouts. The hustle mythology no longer enamors you. You're wiser now. You know what it takes to sustain obsession, and you don't waste energy pretending otherwise.

That wisdom shows up in how you plan, how you recover, and how you lead. You build more margin into your systems. Not to do less, but to do deeper. You start thinking in decades, not quarters. In principles, not tactics. You become less addicted to speed and more committed to quality.

And in that quality, the second obsession begins to reveal its real gift: peace. Not comfort. Not easy. But peace, the kind that comes from alignment, from systems that match your standards, from work that doesn't depend on emotional highs to feel meaningful. You wake up clear. You move with certainty. You build with grace. Not because the stakes are lower, but because you've raised your foundation.

If the first obsession is about finding your edge, the second is about protecting it. And that protection doesn't look like retreat. It seems like evolution. You no longer need every decision to feel dramatic. You've moved past the theatrics of ambition. You're playing for something else now: permanence. Integrity. Transmission.

The second obsession is when you begin to think beyond yourself. You've proven you can do it alone. Now the question becomes: who can I bring with me? What can I teach? What systems can I codify so that others can operate at this level, not through inspiration, but through design?

That's where impact lives, not in the brilliance of your first performance, but in the architecture of your second. That's where your obsession stops being personal and starts becoming structural. That's when your work becomes a reference point, not just for your peers, but for the next generation of builders who will stand on what you refused to compromise.

The second obsession is not optional. It is the bridge between momentum and meaning. It is the invitation to build a life that doesn't collapse once the first storm has passed. And it is the proof that obsession isn't just a phase. It's a framework. A discipline. A calling.

And if you can answer that call, if you can commit again, this time with clarity, systems, and peace, then you'll discover something the first obsession never had time to offer: permanence.

Chapter 29: Creating Friction

In a world obsessed with accessibility, where ease and inclusivity are prized above all, the idea of deliberately introducing friction feels counterintuitive, even arrogant. But if you're building with strategic obsession, friction isn't your enemy. It's your filter. It protects the integrity of your work by ensuring that only the intended individuals arrive.

This is not about gatekeeping for ego. It's about preserving focus. Because when you make everything easy for everyone, you attract the curious, the casual, the uncommitted. These people consume your time, dilute your feedback loops, and pull energy away from those who are aligned. Obsession requires precision. And precision requires thresholds.

Friction, when used with intention, becomes a strategic tool. It says: This is not for everyone. It's for those who are serious. It's for those who are ready. It's for those who value what this truly is, whether you're building a company, a philosophy, a movement, or a product, the willingness to create friction signals that you're optimizing for resonance, not reach.

Strategic obsession does not seek mass appeal. It seeks clarity of mission. And that clarity means drawing lines. Not to exclude, but to ensure coherence. Because if you don't decide who it's for, the market will. And the market always trends toward the lowest common denominator. That's not where extraordinary work lives. Great work requires boundaries.

Creating friction might mean asking more of your audience than they're used to. It might mean requiring applications, charging premium prices, and withholding access until prerequisites are met. It might mean slow onboarding. Long-term engagement. Deep content that can't be skimmed. All of these are signals, not of elitism, but of intentionality. They say: What's inside is too important to be watered down for convenience.

The paradox is that the right people are drawn to that. They don't resist friction; they trust it. It signals that this is not a commodity. That the builder respects their work enough to protect it. That's what they're stepping into: something built for longevity, not hype. When you create friction for the right people, you're not pushing them away. You're calling them forward.

But most creators fear this. They equate access with value. They think that lowering the bar widens the impact. It doesn't. It flattens it. It creates the illusion of reach while diluting the experience that could've changed someone's trajectory. Strategic obsession resists that temptation. It says: better to go deep with a few than shallow with many.

This requires a shift in posture. Instead of asking, "How do I get more attention?" the obsessed ask, "How do I raise the quality of attention I attract?" That shift is everything. It leads to different decisions, decisions rooted in longevity, trust, and integrity. You start thinking in terms of invitation, not promotion. You start designing your brand, product, or system in ways that speak directly to those who are ready and filter out those who aren't.

Friction, when done right, isn't a barrier. It's a test. A gentle but precise way of saying: this matters. This isn't a dopamine hit. This isn't another disposable product. This is something to be taken seriously. If that repels the wrong people, good. It means the signal is working. And if it attracts the right people more deeply, even better. You've earned not just their attention, but their trust.

Trust built through friction is stronger than trust built through convenience. Because it begins with investment. When someone has to climb even a small hill to access your work, they value it differently. They show up differently. They're more likely to engage, to contribute, to stick. That engagement is what obsession needs to thrive. You're not building a crowd. You're building a culture.

Culture is shaped by what you tolerate. And if you tolerate misalignment, distraction, or surface-level thinking, your culture will reflect it. Strategic obsession refuses to compromise at that level. It builds with the long arc in mind. It knows that every shortcut taken today becomes a cost tomorrow and that the friction you fail to introduce at the start will manifest as dissonance down the line.

So how do you do it well? You start by being honest. About who your work is for. About what it demands. About what it's not. You say it plainly, unapologetically. You reinforce it through your design choices, pricing, language, access points, and pacing. You don't try to make it easier. You try to make it more accurate.

And then you trust the right people to rise. To self-select. To show up not because it was easy, but because it was necessary. And those are the people you can build with. Those are the people who contribute to your loop, your system, your vision. Because they're not here for shortcuts. They're here for depth.

Strategic obsession doesn't just ask, "What are we building?" It asks, "Who are we building it for?" And if the answer is everyone, the honest answer is no one. The clearest, strongest, most enduring movements are always the most specific. They're not afraid to polarize. They know that clear signals create resonance. And resonance is worth more than reach.

In the end, friction is not a flaw. It's a feature. A signal. A standard. When used with discipline, it becomes one of the most powerful tools in the obsessed builder's arsenal, not to keep people out, but to ensure the right ones get in.

Chapter 30: Burn the Whiteboard

There comes a moment in every long-term pursuit where the temptation to start over masquerades as clarity. You're tired. The idea feels stale. The system you meticulously architected now feels limiting. And the whiteboard calls to you, a blank slate, a fresh start, a seductive invitation to reimagine everything.

But obsession doesn't always honour the whiteboard. Sometimes, it burns it.

To burn the whiteboard means to reject the comfort of constant reinvention. It's the refusal to romanticize newness over refinement. It's a declaration that you don't need more ideas; you need more depth. And it's the strategic act of saying, "We're not starting over. We're digging in."

In an age where pivoting is considered a virtue and iteration is synonymous with progress, this posture feels radical. But obsession isn't afraid to be radical if it means protecting the mission. Burning the whiteboard doesn't mean abandoning adaptability; it means rejecting distraction disguised as creativity. It's a line in the sand between growth and drift.

The reality is, most people don't burn the whiteboard. They worship it. They treat it like a solution when it's often an escape. When things get hard, they erase instead of refining. They move laterally, chasing the high of novelty instead of the rigour of completion. But obsession knows the difference. Obsession understands that not every uncomfortable system needs to be replaced; some need to be rebuilt from the inside, not wiped clean.

Burning the whiteboard requires courage. It means facing the work that still needs doing, not running from it. It means holding the line on your original commitments, not because they're sentimental, but because they're strategic. There's a cost to every reset, every pivot, every "what if we just…" conversation. And if you're not counting that cost, you're paying it unquestioningly.

Strategic obsession knows when to evolve and when to hold fast. That discernment is rare, especially in organizations or individuals addicted to innovation theatre, where brainstorming sessions are confused for momentum, and constant change is celebrated more than cumulative progress. But the obsessed aren't playing for perception. They're playing for permanence.

There's a difference between iteration and abandonment. Iteration says, "Let's make this better." Abandonment says, "Let's forget we ever tried." One sharpens. The other scatters. The obsessed iterate. The restless abandon. And often, the only way to tell which camp you're in is by watching your relationship to the whiteboard.

The whiteboard loves to promise possibilities. That's its greatest strength, and its most dangerous flaw. Possibility without constraint is chaos. Strategic obsession thrives not in boundless potential, but in focused execution. It says: here is the mission, here is the path, and until we've exhausted it, we are not changing course.

Burning the whiteboard is an act of creative war. It says: we are not seduced by the illusion of reset. We are committed to delivering on our promises, even when it's hard. Especially when it's hard. Because depth takes time, mastery takes iteration. And both are incompatible with constant reinvention.

This mindset isn't rigid. It's principled. It allows for adaptation within boundaries. It permits refinement but resists erosion. It invites new thinking without discarding what's working. That balance is subtle. And it can only be maintained by leaders and creators who know the difference between progress and panic.

In practice, burning the whiteboard might look like cancelling another strategy meeting designed to brainstorm yet another brand positioning, when the current one hasn't even been adequately tested. It might look like shelving a rebrand that was born out of boredom, not data. It might look like forcing yourself to finish the product, the book, the campaign, not because it's perfect, but because it's aligned with the mission you committed to when you had clarity.

And when you do that, when you resist the reset, you discover something rare: compounding. The quiet power that comes from staying in motion on the same idea, with the same rigour, under increasing pressure. Most never feel that power because they hit eject too early. They tell themselves the concept was flawed. But it wasn't flawed, it was just unpolished. And polish takes grit.

The whiteboard is a tool. But like any tool, it can become a crutch. Burn it when it starts whispering escape. Burn it when it makes you doubt every system you've tested. Burn it when it offers the fantasy of clarity without the cost of effort.

What emerges in its absence is focus. And from that focus, endurance. And from that endurance, obsession, not with newness, but with truth. Not with stimulation, but with sovereignty. You're not building something that looks fresh. You're creating something that works.

In the end, there will always be another whiteboard. Another clean slate. Another chance to erase. But those who finish, those who break through, are not the ones who chase reset. They are the ones who burn the whiteboard, sharpen their tools, and get back to the work.

Chapter 31: Signals, Not Noise

The world is not short on information. It's drowning in it. Metrics, feedback, opinions, updates, endless streams of data, most of it loud and urgent but ultimately irrelevant. The noise is constant, and for the undisciplined, it's paralyzing. Every ping feels important. Every dashboard spike demands interpretation. Every comment becomes a referendum on direction.

But strategic obsession doesn't get hijacked by noise. It's tuned for a signal.

Signal is what matters. Signal is what aligns. It's the thread of truth running through the chaos. The pattern beneath the surface. The insight that moves the work forward. But the signal doesn't scream. It doesn't flash or trend or announce itself with fanfare. The signal is quiet. Subtle. And that's why it's missed by most people who are moving too fast, checking too often, optimizing too early.

To chase a signal, you must build filters. Internal ones first. You must know what you're optimizing for, what you believe in. What matters to your mission more than momentum or applause? Without those filters, everything feels important. You'll find yourself reacting instead of building, pulled toward every opinion that confirms your doubt or flatters your ego.

The obsessed don't have time for that. Their attention is too precious. They treat it like a capital. Deployed deliberately, evaluated constantly, guarded aggressively. They know that focus is their most valuable asset, and distraction is their most reliable enemy. And so, they stop letting noise masquerade as urgency.

That discipline begins with metrics. In a digital world, you can track everything. But just because you can doesn't mean you should. Strategic obsession asks: Which metrics are *directional*? Which numbers reflect behaviour, resonance, depth, not just reach or velocity? Surface metrics, such as followers, impressions, and bounce rates, can be manipulated, gamed, or misinterpreted. Signal metrics go deeper. Retention. Return visits. Referral without incentive. These show whether your work is not just being seen but remembered. Trusted and acted upon.

The same applies to feedback. Not all feedback is created equal. Most of it is reactive, uncalibrated, or driven by the insecurities of the person giving it. Obsession doesn't absorb feedback indiscriminately. It categorizes it. It asks: Is this feedback coming from someone inside the arena or watching from the sidelines? Do they understand the mission? Are they qualified to comment on this layer of the work?

Signals often come from the quietest sources, loyal users who don't post about you but never leave, team members who solve the same problem twice without being told, moments when a system performs under pressure without needing attention. The unsexy proof points. The ones that don't get shared in investor updates but hold the real weight of long-term success.

This posture toward signal is not just intellectual; it's emotional. It requires emotional discipline to ignore noise that flatters. To reject urgency that isn't real. To stay committed when the loudest voices in the room are calling for change. That's what makes the obsessed dangerous. Not their energy, but their clarity. Not their volume, but their fidelity to signal.

Noise will always outnumber the signal. That's why attention is such a powerful form of leverage. Most people squander their time reacting to the wrong things. The obsessed refine theirs, narrowing their bandwidth to a razor's edge, focusing only on what compounds. They know that every glance, every distraction, every notification clicked is a vote cast for mediocrity.

To operate this way requires design. It requires that you actively reduce your noise exposure not just through willpower, but through systems. Default off instead of default on. One screen instead of five. Fewer inputs. Clearer priorities. Environments that reward deep work, not dopamine loops.

Teams that build around signal move differently. They have fewer meetings. Clearer dashboards. Less performative urgency. They're not flailing in the face of every tweet or trend. They're tracking movement where it matters. This isn't slowness, it's precision—and precision compounds.

At the personal level, this approach liberates you from the tyranny of constant comparison. You stop measuring your pace against those optimizing for visibility. You stop reacting to the false urgency of someone else's crisis. You no longer need to prove your direction every 48 hours. You know what you're doing. You know why it matters. And you don't need applause to keep going.

This doesn't mean becoming blind or rigid. Signals evolve. Markets shift. Assumptions must be tested. But the testing is done on purpose, not as a reaction, but as an investigation. The obsessed are not closed-minded. They're selectively permeable. They let in what sharpens, not what shakes.

What emerges from this posture is resilience. Not the kind that grits through everything blindly, but the type that can distinguish between helpful feedback and noise pollution. Between a signal to pivot and a flare of momentary discomfort. Between urgency that's real and urgency that's manufactured.

And as the noise increases, as the world gets louder, faster, more reactive, this skill becomes a superpower. The ability to hold your focus, to stay anchored to your signal, to build even while others panic or pivot or preach. That is what separates the enduring from the exhausted.

In the end, obsession isn't about doing more. It's about hearing more clearly, seeing more sharply, and knowing what to ignore so you can honour what matters. And in a world that can't stop screaming, the ones who win will be those who can still hear the signal in the silence.

Chapter 32: Radical Ownership

There is no obsession without ownership. Not the shallow kind, where you take credit when things go well and disappear when they don't. Not the polished kind, where optics matter more than integrity. Strategic obsession requires something more profound. More demanding. More confronting. It requires radical ownership, the kind that rewires how you think about responsibility, results, and reality itself.

Radical ownership begins with one assumption: **if it's in your orbit, it's yours**. Every missed deadline, every unclear message, every broken system, every underperformance on your team, even when others are involved, is, at least in part, your responsibility. Not because you caused it directly, but because you could have influenced it. Anticipated it. Designed around it. Intervened sooner. Communicated better.

Most people resist this level of ownership. They want to compartmentalize it. They'll own their effort, but not the outcome. They'll take credit for clarity, but not confusion. But obsession doesn't give you that out. When you're strategically obsessed, you're not just executing within a system; you *are* the system. Your inputs create your environment. Your actions shape your outcomes. And your refusal to own that truth is the quickest way to stall.

Radical ownership doesn't mean you blame yourself for everything. It means you *respond* to everything. You don't waste time in defensiveness. You move to solve. To strengthen. To fix. Your instinct isn't "Who did this?" It's "What needs to happen now?" That shift, from blame to responsibility, is the mark of someone building something that lasts.

This posture eliminates excuses. Not because life is fair, but because excuses are useless. They don't change outcomes. They don't build systems. They don't create clarity. All they do is buy comfort. And obsession doesn't prioritize comfort; it prioritizes movement.

In practice, radical ownership manifests in small, brutal ways. You rewrite the sloppy sentence. You catch the flaw in your product before the customer does. You show up to the call even when you're tired. You answer the uncomfortable question without hedging. You hold the line on your standards when no one's watching. Because all of those moments compound into trust, trust from others, yes, but more importantly, trust in yourself.

You start to believe in your effectiveness, not as a mood, but as a pattern. And that belief fuels speed. When you own everything, you don't wait for permission. You don't defer upward. You act. You move. You adjust in real time. And that agility makes you dangerous in the best way possible.

But this level of ownership comes with weight. It's heavy. It can't be offloaded to a consultant or hidden behind a brand. If the project's wrong, you fix it. If the team's off, you lead them. If the direction is unclear, you sit down and do the hard thinking until it isn't. Ownership means you stop outsourcing your clarity.

And perhaps most importantly, radical ownership includes *emotional ownership*. You don't just manage tasks. You manage your state. You don't blame others for your distraction, your burnout, your lack of creativity. You study your rhythms. You build your day around peak focus. You engineer your inputs. You learn how to reset, recharge, and return to work faster. You don't expect someone else to maintain your edge for you.

This is the kind of discipline that terrifies average operators. They're waiting for ideal conditions. They need a manager, a mentor, and a market shift to give them momentum. The obsessed aren't waiting. They build the momentum themselves, through ownership. Through daily confrontation. Through the refusal to be anything less than responsible for everything they touch.

And in that ownership, something powerful happens: you become sovereign. Untouchable by excuses. Immune to stagnation. Because you're not waiting for circumstances to improve, you're becoming the kind of person who improves them. That posture translates. Others notice. And they begin to expect more from themselves in your presence.

Teams led by individuals with a radical obsession operate with a different cadence. They move faster, not because they're rushed, but because there's no time wasted on ambiguity. They solve problems without the safety net of blame. They operate with cleaner inputs, tighter loops, and higher standards, not because someone enforces them, but because someone models them.

This creates culture. Not the kind you print on posters, but the kind that shapes behaviour. Ownership is contagious. It sharpens everyone close enough to feel it. And it creates separation, the type of separation that's hard to replicate, because it isn't technical. It's personal.

Radical ownership is not about being the hero. It's not about martyrdom or self-punishment. It's about clarity. About confronting reality without flinching. About refusing to let anything, anything, be "not your problem." It's the posture that says: *if it touches my mission, I will handle it.* Fully. Quietly. Completely.

And in a world obsessed with delegation, diffusion, and distance, that posture is rare. It's also magnetic. Because in the end, people don't follow perfection; they follow responsibility. They trust the builder who doesn't flinch when things go wrong. Who doesn't deflect? Who doesn't hide? Who says: *I've got it. Let's fix it.*

Radical ownership is the final layer of obsession. It's what makes the rest of it real. Without it, all the clarity, all the focus, all the ambition amount to potential. With it, everything becomes kinetic. Strategic. Inevitable.

Chapter 33: Obsession Without Burnout

To the outside world, obsession and burnout often look like close cousins. The long hours, the narrowed focus, the ruthless prioritization, they can all blur into a narrative of collapse. We've been taught to fear intensity, to treat sustained effort as inherently unsustainable. But the truth is more nuanced. Obsession doesn't cause burnout. *Poorly managed* obsession does.

Burnout is not the result of doing too much. It's the result of doing too much that doesn't matter. Or worse, doing too much without understanding *why* it matters. When the effort is disconnected from meaning, from momentum, from progress, your energy drains faster than it replenishes. You're not just tired. You're disoriented.

The strategically obsessed don't burn out because of volume. They burn out when they lose alignment, when their systems break. When their signal fades, that's when the grind turns toxic, when motion is decoupled from purpose.

To build obsessively without burning out, you must engineer for sustainability from the beginning. Not after the breakdown. Not when you hit the wall. From day one. That means designing your operating system to create *regenerative tension*, not just pressure. It means understanding how to work hard without bleeding into self-destruction. And that takes strategy.

The first strategic shift is this: redefine rest as part of the work.

The obsessed don't rest to escape the mission. They rest to *serve* it. They understand that recovery isn't a luxury, it's a lever.

It sharpens clarity. It preserves focus. It reduces rework. Rest is not the enemy of obsession. It's what allows obsession to endure.

But rest, in this context, isn't passive. It's not scrolling on a couch, numbing out with content. It's intentional disconnection. Movement. Stillness. Practices that allow the nervous system to downshift without collapse. Rituals that cleanse attention, not fragment it. Sleep, solitude, nature, reflection, these are strategic acts when you're building at the edge of your capacity.

Second, the obsessed build *boundaries*, not balance.

Balance implies even distribution. But obsession isn't balanced. It's weighted. Intentionally. You can't devote your life to something and give equal bandwidth to everything else. That's not sustainable, it's dishonest. But boundaries? Boundaries are how you protect the mission *and* yourself.

A boundary might be as simple as no notifications after 7 PM. Or no meetings before 11 AM. It might mean clearing one full day each week for deep work or deep rest. It might mean saying no to networking, socializing, or pseudo-opportunities that dilute focus. These aren't acts of selfishness. They're acts of stewardship. You're protecting the vessel. You're safeguarding the system.

Third, they optimize their environment for energy, not just productivity.

Burnout creeps in when your environment creates friction instead of flow. When your tools, your calendar, and your workspace are out of sync with how you work best. The obsessed don't tolerate default settings. They shape their environments like they shape their minds, deliberately, constantly.

This includes lighting. Sound. Temperature. Ergonomics. Digital hygiene. It involves working in environments where you're least likely to be interrupted and structuring your day around peak cognitive windows. It includes building a space that feeds your rhythm, not fights it.

Fourth, they observe themselves like engineers, not martyrs.

Strategic obsession requires self-inquiry. Not just "How am I feeling?" but "What's working? What's lagging? What patterns are emerging?" This is not navel-gazing. It's diagnostics. You treat your focus like a performance system. You measure your inputs and outputs. You track energy, not just time. You intervene early. You treat your body and mind as sacred instruments, because they are.

That might mean shifting your sleep schedule, adjusting your nutrition, and rethinking your stimulant use. Cycling between sprint and recovery phases. None of this is about optimization for optimization's sake. It's about *durability*. Because obsession isn't a phase, it's a mode. And modes must be sustained.

Fifth, they allow their identity to evolve.

Burnout often emerges when you cling to a version of yourself that no longer fits. When you keep trying to produce at a level that made sense two years ago, under entirely different conditions. The obsessed don't freeze their identity. They grow it. They stay sensitive to internal shifts. They know when to delegate. When to retool. When to slow down, not out of weakness, but because the mission demands a new kind of output.

Finally, and maybe most crucially: the obsessed *build for meaning*.

Burnout thrives in meaningless output. In work that's performative, disconnected, or built for someone else's scoreboard. The obsessed are insulated from this because they've chosen a path they believe in. Their work may be challenging, but it's *aligned*. That alignment creates resilience. They can weather intensity because they're anchored in purpose. They can endure long hours because they see the point. They don't need external praise to feel energized, because the work itself returns energy.

That's the real secret to obsession without burnout: obsession that returns more than it takes. Not every day. Not every cycle. But across the arc. A mission that feeds you as you feed it. A pursuit that sharpens you, even as it demands more from you. A system that adapts as you evolve, rather than requiring you to shrink to fit it.

Burnout is not a symptom of ambition. It's a symptom of disconnection. From self. From strategy. From signal. Obsession, when built deliberately, heals that disconnection. It draws you back to the center. It gives your days shape. It reminds you that intensity is not the problem. Misalignment is.

So, build your systems. Protect your rhythm. Trust your internal diagnostics. And remember: the goal is not balance. The goal is longevity. The goal is to be still building with clarity, intensity, and peace, ten years from now.

Chapter 34: Designing for the Long Game

The world is obsessed with the short term. Headlines cycle by the hour. Product launches are measured in weeks. Careers pivot every quarter. Even attention spans have been compressed to the length of a reel. In this climate, long-term thinking isn't just rare, it's radical. But for the strategically obsessed, it's non-negotiable.

To build something that lasts, you must first **decide** that you're playing the long game. That decision changes everything. It changes how you allocate time, what risks you take, what feedback you ignore, and what metrics you measure. It shifts your posture from urgency to intention, from reaction to architecture. You stop sprinting and start constructing.

The long game requires more than patience. It demands **design**. Not just vague ambition or hopeful consistency, but systems engineered to carry you through seasons. Through reinventions. Through the inevitable dips, droughts, and detours. Strategic obsession isn't about holding one idea forever. It's about having the *discipline* to evolve the mission without abandoning the foundation.

The first component of long-game design is the **durability of vision**. Your vision cannot be so brittle that it snaps under pressure, nor so vague that it dilutes under scrutiny. It needs to be rooted in principle, not just preference. A good long-term vision is directional but flexible. It allows for iteration without erasing your identity.

You don't need to know exactly what your brand, platform, or idea will look like in ten years. But you do need to know what *won't* change. What values are non-negotiable? What audience are you serving, even if the delivery mechanism evolves? What problem will still matter when the current trend fades? Those are your anchors. And long games are won by those who build from anchors, not aesthetics.

The second principle is **delayed optimization**. The long game punishes premature optimization. If you scale a fragile system, you multiply its weaknesses. If you monetize too early, you risk building around short-term incentives. The strategically obsessed resist this. They allow time for the thing to *become what it's meant to become*, not what it can cash flow in the next fiscal quarter.

That means tolerating ambiguity, manually repeating processes before automating them, and withholding growth levers until the backend is unbreakable. The obsessed know that polishing a product too soon locks in assumptions. And if those assumptions are wrong, every layer built on top of them becomes technical and philosophical debt.

Designing for the long game also requires **flexible architecture**. Rigidity is a liability. You need systems that evolve with you, not ones that fossilize. That means building modular products that can be expanded, ideas that can be reframed, and audiences that grow with you rather than age out of relevance.

This isn't about being everything to everyone. It's about building with enough margin that your obsession can adapt without losing its shape. Long games reward those who can pivot without panic. Who can adjust their message, their medium, even their model, while still holding the mission.

Another layer of long-game design is **relationship compounding**. In short-term games, people are transactions. In long games, people are infrastructure. Every customer is a signal. Every employee is a multiplier. Every partner is a strategic layer.

The obsessed treat these relationships like equity. They invest early. They over-deliver. They don't burn bridges because they know the person you ignored today might be the gatekeeper of the opportunity you'll need in five years. They build reputations slowly, with intention. And they let trust grow at the speed of real outcomes, not branding.

Long-game players also have a different relationship with **timing**. They aren't addicted to momentum. They know that seasons of deep work, invisibility, or recalibration are not threats; they're necessary. The obsession with design for these valleys. They don't interpret every slowdown as a signal of failure. They use the time to sharpen, to simplify, to set the conditions for a leap that will come later.

This is why designing for the long game includes a **cash flow strategy**. You cannot play long if you're financially fragile. Obsession doesn't flourish in desperation. It needs enough stability to make the non-obvious move. To say no to good opportunities to protect great ones. To build slow, strong foundations instead of chasing fast, flimsy wins.

The long game also requires **emotional durability, which** means building support systems. Not just therapists or coaches, but friends who understand the arc. Partners who support the quiet years. Teams that don't panic when growth flattens. A mind that can differentiate between boredom and misalignment.

And above all, designing for the long game means **designing your identity** to evolve. You won't be the same person in five years. You'll need new skills. New routines. New self-concepts. Obsession allows for that. It doesn't trap you in a fixed posture. It gives you something more profound to carry across versions of yourself: *a mission*.

Because at the heart of all long games is belief. Not unquestioning optimism. Not naïve hustle. But the belief that your best work compounds, not just in metrics, but in meaning. That staying aligned is more valuable than staying visible. That building slowly, well, and with conviction is not a risk; it's the advantage.

The market will reward the frantic in spurts. But it will always reward the focused in the long run. The person who designed for decade-scale outcomes. Who resisted premature acceleration. Who built something people return to, not because it's trendy, but because it's *true*.

Play that game. Design that system. Become that person.

Chapter 35: The Obsession Feedback Loop

Sustainable obsession isn't powered by adrenaline or novelty. It's powered by a loop, a self-reinforcing system that strengthens itself over time. When designed well, this feedback loop becomes the engine of long-term focus. It transforms obsession from an emotional state into an operational advantage.

Most people treat feedback as a moment. A one-time response. A performance review. A comment section. A survey. But obsession doesn't thrive on moments; it thrives on **loops**. Continuous, calibrated, high-fidelity feedback that informs, sharpens, and evolves the work in real time.

The feedback loop that drives obsession is built from four components: **output, signal, interpretation, and adjustment**. It begins with deliberate output, not just action, but action rooted in clarity. You're not just throwing ideas into the void. You're building something with intent. A product. A post. A message. A feature. A system. Each output is a probe into the world. A question disguised as creation: Does this land?

But output alone means nothing without a signal. Signal is the response, not just the loud response, but the true one. It shows up in behaviour more than words. Did people stay? Did they return? Did they take action? Did the right people resonate, or did you attract noise? Signal tells you what reality thinks of your assumptions.

Then comes interpretation. This is the most fragile point in the loop. Because most people misread the signal, they personalize it.

They overreact. They dismiss the quiet truths and obsess over the loud noise. But the obsessed interpret the signal *strategically*. They don't take it personally. They take it seriously.

They ask: What part of this feedback is valuable? What does it say about the alignment between my intent and my impact? Are we hitting the right nerve? Are we speaking to the right audience? Do we need to refine the message, the product, or the timing? This is not guesswork. It's an analysis—pattern recognition. Strategic calibration.

And finally, adjustment. You shift. You edit. You double down. You trim. But you don't start over. You don't abandon the mission. You don't react emotionally. You adjust like a sniper, not a demolition crew. The feedback loop isn't designed to keep you reinventing. It's designed to keep you evolving.

The faster you can move through this loop, without rushing, without skipping steps, the sharper your work becomes. The more you build not just for the market, but *with* it. You become iterative without losing identity. You become responsive without becoming reactive.

But to keep this loop alive, you need structure. Feedback doesn't just arrive cleanly. It must be captured, categorized, and fed into the system. The obsessed build mechanisms for this. Systems that track real engagement, not vanity metrics. Processes that collect qualitative feedback from high-value users. Tools that highlight what's working *and* what's unclear.

These systems are lightweight but powerful. A simple tagging system on support tickets. A weekly synthesis of user comments. A short voice memo log where ideas get reviewed each Friday.

You don't need enterprise software. You need *discipline*. Rituals that keep you listening while still building.

The feedback loop also relies on **trust**, both in the system and in yourself. You must trust that consistent, honest input will sharpen the work. And you must trust yourself to interpret that input without bias. That means eliminating ego as a filter. When someone doesn't resonate, it doesn't mean you failed. It means you received information. That information is power, if you let it be.

Too many talented people destroy their loops with defensiveness. They provide feedback about identity instead of alignment. The obsessed never forget: you are not your product. You are not your last launch. You are the builder. And your job is not to be right, it's to get closer to what's true.

Over time, this loop becomes internalized. You start thinking about feedback. You begin to hear the signal before it's spoken. You anticipate the market's questions because you've seen the pattern so many times. This is the compounding effect of obsession; it makes you not just more productive, but *more accurate*.

Accuracy creates speed. Because you stop wasting energy on guesses. You stop building for imagined audiences. You stop solving problems that aren't real. Your loop keeps you honest. It trims your drift. It turns every output into an experiment that sharpens your next one.

And here's the beautiful part: the more accurate you become, the more trust you earn. From users. From teams. From markets. Your hit rate improves. Your instincts get sharper. Not because you're magical, but because your loop is.

Eventually, the loop creates something rare: **momentum that doesn't rely on mood**. You don't need motivation to start. You need a signal. And you've built a system that keeps delivering it. You're not just creating, you're *learning while creating*. And learning is the fuel of sustainable obsession.

This loop protects you from burnout. It protects you from delusion. It protects you from stagnation. It keeps you moving, not just forward, but toward something sharper, truer, and more aligned. You're not just working hard. You're working in a system that upgrades itself.

And that's the point. Strategic obsession isn't just about passion. It's about precision. And precision is built through feedback, not once, not occasionally, but perpetually. The obsessed know this. They don't fear feedback. They *design* it. They honour the loop. They feed it with clarity. And they trust it to return insight.

When you build your loop, you're no longer guessing. You're compounding. And in a world of noise, iteration, and performance, that is your advantage.

Chapter 36: Decentralize the Mission

Every mission that aims to scale, whether a business, a movement, a philosophy, or a product, must eventually face a painful tension: how do you grow beyond yourself without losing the clarity that started it all? How do you delegate action while preserving direction? How do you let go of control while holding onto essence?

This is where most great work begins to fracture. Founders become bottlenecks. Teams dilute purpose. Users drift from core principles. The reason isn't lack of talent or intent; it's lack of architectural thinking. The difference between expansion and entropy lies in one critical distinction: **decentralize the mission, never the vision**.

To decentralize the mission means to distribute ownership of *execution*. It means creating systems and people that can carry the work forward without requiring your daily intervention. It means empowering others to solve problems, make decisions, and take initiative. And it's the only way to escape the gravitational pull of your involvement.

But vision? That cannot be decentralized. Not if you want to protect the soul of the work.

Vision is the thread that holds everything together. It's the operating system beneath every action, every decision, every iteration. It's the clarity about *why* this matters, *for whom*, and *what it refuses to compromise on*. Without vision, decentralization becomes diffusion. Everyone pulls in slightly different directions, slowly eroding what made the work powerful in the first place.

This is the paradox of obsession: the more committed you are to the long-term mission, the more you must invite others in, but the more carefully you must protect the thing that can't be compromised.

To do this well requires structure. You must **codify the vision** in a way that is easily communicated. It cannot live only in your head. It cannot be a feeling, a vibe, a founder myth. It must be expressible, clear, consistent, and concrete. That means writing it down and clarifying the boundaries. Defining what success *is* and *is not*. Naming the values, the voice, the customers you serve, and making invisible standards visible.

Great organizations do this early. Obsessive ones revisit it constantly. Because as teams grow and roles expand, the gravitational force pulling people away from first principles gets stronger. Vision begins to drift, not maliciously, but subtly. And unless you've created a mechanism to regularly re-anchor it, your team will slowly become efficient at executing the wrong things.

The obsessed prevent this by creating what we might call **vision rituals**. These are lightweight, repeatable practices that keep the center strong. They might resemble onboarding documents that reveal the story behind the strategy, rather than just the roadmap. Weekly team reviews that connect execution to purpose. Leadership standups that ask not just "what are we building?" but "are we still aligned?"

These rituals are not performative. They're protective. They prevent the slow erosion of coherence. Because once coherence is lost, everything feels off. Product decisions get weirder.

Messaging becomes brittle. The team starts asking for clarity that used to be implicit. These are not signs of growth; they are signs of vision slippage.

But vision protection is not about rigidity. It's about **principled flexibility**. You must design systems that allow teams to explore, iterate, and even experiment without drifting from the core. That means defining what's sacred and what's flexible. Sacred might be: who we serve, how we speak, and what we never compromise. Flexible might be: pricing, packaging, features, tactics.

That distinction lets people move with freedom without accidentally breaking the foundation. It encourages innovation *within* established boundaries, rather than pushing people to the edges where clarity is lost.

When you decentralize the mission but not the vision, you also create **strategic leverage**. Your time becomes magnified. You no longer need to be in every room, but your thinking shows up in every decision. You're not micromanaging outcomes, you're curating context. The work moves faster but still moves true.

This is what separates obsessive builders from reactive leaders. The reactive either hoards control (and burns out) or delegates everything (and drifts). The obsessed design a system where the *doing* is distributed, but the *direction* is unmistakable.

This design also creates resilience. Because vision-centric systems can withstand turnover, volatility, and even crisis. When people leave, the mission doesn't vanish. When trends shift, your essence doesn't collapse. When growth brings complexity, you don't lose the signal in the noise. The vision holds. And everything reorients around it.

For this to work, though, you must make peace with letting go of ego. You don't need to be the hero. You don't need to touch every decision. You don't even need to be the most visible voice. You need to be the steward of clarity. The one who refuses to let the original conviction get diluted in pursuit of scale.

And here's the beauty: when you do this right, your vision becomes *amplified*, not diminished. Others start articulating it in new ways. They adapt it to contexts you never considered. They take it further than you could alone. Not because they've changed it, but because they've internalized it. And now, the mission grows *through* them, not *because* of you.

Strategic obsession scales through culture. And culture is nothing more than vision, lived consistently. You don't need a hundred policies. You need ten sentences that explain *why* you're here, and the discipline to build everything else around them.

Decentralize the mission. Let others carry the weight. Design systems that distribute action. But protect the vision. Not by locking it away, but by making it so clear, so resonant, so embedded, that it doesn't need protection. It travels on its own.

That's how you build something that outlives you, not just in brand, but in belief. That's how you play long. That's how obsession becomes a legacy.

Chapter 37: The Rhythm of Obsession

Obsession is often misunderstood as a frenzy, an endless sprint fueled by adrenaline and panic. But those who sustain it over the years know better. Obsession, real obsession, has a rhythm. It is not chaotic. It is not erratic. It moves like a pulse, steady, self-renewing, and deliberate.

To build obsessively is to discover and harness your rhythm. And rhythm isn't just about productivity. It's about *resonance*, with your energy, your environment, your priorities. It is the invisible metronome that keeps your work alive without tearing you apart. Most people burn out because they never find this rhythm. They push when they should rest. They slow down when they should surge. They confuse movement with momentum, wondering why nothing compounds.

Rhythm begins with **awareness**. Strategic obsession is not just about working hard; it's about knowing *when* you work best, *how* you work best, and *why* that pattern serves your larger goal. This is not a motivational tactic. It's a diagnostic one. The obsessed don't guess at their cycles. They study them.

You learn your rhythm by observing the patterns in your daily data. When are you sharpest? What time of day does your deep work peak? When do distractions creep in? What rituals calm you? What triggers resistance? You track energy, not just effort. And over time, a pattern emerges, a rhythm that, once honoured, returns more than it takes.

This rhythm is not one-size-fits-all. Some builders wake at 4 a.m. and attack the morning. Others find their genius in midnight silence. Some sprint in four-hour blocks. Others stack small, intentional steps throughout the day. Obsession doesn't care when you work. It cares whether your *system works*. And systems that work are built in sync with rhythm.

Once you know your rhythm, the next step is to **design around it**. That means engineering your environment, your calendar, your commitments to serve the rhythm, not sabotage it. This might mean saying no to morning meetings and or clearing entire afternoons. Or batching similar work on specific days. Rhythm demands constraint. Not rigidity, but *clarity*. If everything is a possibility, rhythm dies. If priorities are fixed, rhythm thrives.

Designing for rhythm also means accounting for the *phases* of obsession. Because obsession does not flow evenly, it moves in cycles, sprints, and stillness, surges, and synthesis. Most builders ignore this. They try to maintain the same output in all seasons. But obsession honours seasonality. It knows when to drive and when to digest.

There are seasons of **deep production**, when you're building, creating, shipping, solving. The pace is high, the pressure real. In these moments, rhythm means holding the line: protecting time, preserving clarity, reducing noise. There's little room for socializing, multitasking, or shallow distraction. These are sacred weeks, and you build your life to protect them.

Then come seasons of **review and recalibration**. These are less glamorous. Less shareable. But they are where the next surge is born. In these moments, rhythm means stepping back, not to quit, but to refine. You audit the work. You re-clarify the vision.

You reset the systems. And you resist the urge to chase dopamine while your strategy matures.

There are also seasons of **strategic slowness**. Not laziness. Not stagnation. Slowness. These are the pauses between waves, the silence before the breakthrough. Most fear these. They panic when motion stalls. But the obsessed know that stillness is not the absence of progress; it is where a new rhythm is composed. It's where ideas are distilled, where resilience is restored.

To maintain rhythm through all of this, the obsessed rely on **rituals**. Rituals are not routines. Routines can become robotic. Rituals are intentional. They are anchored in meaning. A morning walk not for steps, but for orientation. A weekly review not for formality, but for realignment. A writing sprint, a reset day, a screen-free Sunday, whatever protects the pulse of your work.

These rituals function like beats. They divide time into manageable cadences. They give shape to chaos. They help you re-enter flow without waiting for motivation. And most importantly, they remind you that rhythm is a choice, not a gift. You do not find rhythm. You build it.

Rhythm also plays a role in **collaboration**. Teams that build well together do so not because they're all intense, but because their rhythms are compatible. They communicate in sync. They respect one another's peak hours, energy flows, and need for space. Obsession at the team level becomes possible when rhythm is synchronized.

This synchronization doesn't require uniformity. It requires visibility. When everyone understands how others work, the collaboration becomes rhythmic, not reactive. Meetings shrink.

Friction drops. Creativity rises. Teams stop interrupting and start *resonating*. The system becomes smarter than the sum of its parts.

And yet, for all its structure, rhythm must remain *adaptable because* obsession evolves—life shifts. Your seasons change. What worked two years ago may feel brittle now. Rhythm isn't a trap; it's a tether. It must move with you. And the obsessed update their systems the way musicians tune their instruments: regularly, intuitively, relentlessly.

Ultimately, the rhythm of obsession isn't about hustle. It's about harmony. A harmony between focus and freedom, speed and slowness, solitude and collaboration. It's the infrastructure behind intensity. The discipline behind momentum. The difference between burnout and breakthrough.

To the outsider, this rhythm may look calm. Underwhelming, even. But inside, it's electric. It hums with direction. Every block of time is owned. Every decision echoes. Every day builds, not just forward, but upward. That's how you know obsession is healthy: it doesn't just generate effort. It generates coherence.

So learn your rhythm. Protect it. Sharpen it. Let it carry you through the chaos. Because when you move in rhythm, you don't just produce more, you become *undistractable*. And in a world addicted to noise, that is the final competitive advantage.

Chapter 38: Obsession is a Leadership Strategy

Leadership isn't about charisma. It's not about command, or consensus, or comfort. At its highest level, leadership is about **clarity**, clarity of direction, clarity of standards, and clarity of belief. And no force on earth delivers clarity like obsession.

Strategic obsession isn't just a personal operating system. It's a leadership strategy. When deployed with intention, it shapes the behaviour, psychology, and culture of everyone it touches. Not through force. Not through manipulation. But through gravity. Obsession, when real, when disciplined, when earned, pulls people into alignment.

Because people don't follow instructions, they follow conviction.

A leader who is strategically obsessed doesn't need to preach values every week. They embody them. Their decisions reveal their priorities. Their posture sets the tone. Their work ethic dissolves the need for motivational speeches. The team doesn't guess what matters, because the leader makes it visible in every move.

This is how culture scales, through modelling, not messaging.

But obsession as a leadership strategy only works when it's **anchored**, not weaponized. There's a dangerous version of obsession that masquerades as leadership: performative overwork, unchecked intensity, unrealistic expectations. That's not leadership. That's ego. And it fractures teams.

Real obsession, strategic obsession, creates momentum without manufacturing pressure. It holds the line without holding people hostage. It delivers clarity without killing autonomy. It invites people into a vision that's big enough to matter, but clear enough to follow.

Great leaders know this: people don't burn out from hard work. They burn out from meaningless work. From confusing work. From leadership that demands excellence but refuses to define it. The obsessed fix that by setting *visible standards*. They don't just ask for quality, they *show* what quality looks like. They edit in public. They explain decisions. They build taste through repetition.

That's what makes obsession contagious. Not just its intensity, but its consistency. When a leader applies the same care to the small things as they do to the big ones, people notice. They stop cutting corners. They start paying attention. They begin to see that excellence isn't a phase, it's a pattern.

And that pattern becomes the operating system of the team.

Obsession also sharpens leadership by collapsing the gap between **vision and action**. Many leaders live in abstraction. They talk about the future, the mission, the why, but they never touch the work. The obsessed don't hide behind strategy. They shape it with their hands. They operate close to the problem. Close to the customer. Close to the consequence.

This proximity gives them credibility. It also gives them accuracy. They're not making decisions from a mountaintop. They're iterating from the ground. And their teams feel that. They trust decisions that come from exposure. They follow leaders who are in it with them, not above it.

Obsession also changes how leaders handle **conflict**. Most avoid it. They soften it. They delay the complicated conversation in the name of morale. But the obsessed know that avoidance is corrosive. That misalignment, if left unspoken, spreads. They don't lead by emotion. They lead by standards. And when the standard is missed, they address it, not with shame, but with specificity.

They make feedback normal. Regular. Expected. Not just when something's broken, but as part of the operating rhythm. This keeps the system clean. No unspoken resentments. No ambiguity about expectations. Just clear loops. Tight cycles. Shared truth.

That's another reason obsession scales: it brings *truth to the surface*. When a leader is obsessed with reality, when they chase signals, measure honestly, and respond precisely, everyone else becomes sharper too. The whole team learns to respect truth more than comfort. To prioritize learning over ego. That posture is rare. It's also magnetic.

Over time, obsession transforms leadership into **alignment**. Not the kind enforced through hierarchy, but the kind earned through resonance. The team starts to feel like a cohesive unit. Inputs lead to predictable outputs. Roles are clear. Confusion shrinks. And energy compounds, because no one is wasting it on guessing, explaining, or recovering from poor decisions.

But none of this happens if the obsession is performative. Suppose it's just a mask for control. Or a shortcut for influence. Strategic obsession is only a leadership advantage if it's real. Lived. And *strategic*.

That means it's directed toward a mission larger than the self. It serves the work, not the ego. It inspires autonomy, not dependence. It doesn't demand loyalty; it earns it through consistency, clarity, and courage.

Courage is a keyword here. Because to lead through obsession is to lead with relentless honesty. You confront the drift. You admit when the vision is fuzzy. You change direction publicly when you realize you were wrong. And you do it all with posture, not panic.

Teams follow that. They don't expect perfection. They expect *ownership*. Obsession delivers that in spades. Because the obsessed don't wait for someone else to fix it. If it's broken, they fix it. If it's unclear, they clarify it. If it's urgent, they act.

When you lead this way, something unexpected happens: your team begins to adopt the obsession, not as mimicry, but as muscle. They take initiative. They self-correct. They raise their standards without being asked. Because they're no longer just working under a leader, they're working *inside a vision*.

That's the mark of strategic leadership. Not a cult of personality. Not a hierarchy of dependence. But a system of shared clarity, sustained by obsession, and guided by someone who understands that the point of leadership isn't to be followed, it's to build others who can *lead themselves*.

Obsession, when wielded wisely, builds those kinds of teams. Those kinds of systems. Those kinds of outcomes.

So, if you want to lead, don't start with tactics. Start with belief. Obsess over the mission. Protect its clarity. Model its standards. And trust that the rest will follow, not because you demand it, but because you made it undeniable.

Chapter 39: The Obsession Dividend

There comes a point in every long-term pursuit where the results begin to outpace the effort. Not because the effort has decreased, but because the *system* has matured. This inflection point is what we call the **Obsession Dividend**, the exponential return on years of focused, disciplined, strategically obsessive work.

Most people never reach it. Not because they lack talent or vision, but because they quit before compounding can take hold. They pivot too early, spread too thin, or grow distracted just before the reward arrives. Obsession, when consistent and calibrated, pushes you past that danger zone. It keeps you moving when logic says to stop. And on the other side, something rare happens: the system starts to return more than it costs.

The Obsession Dividend is not a moment. It's a phase shift—a sustained increase in return per unit of effort. Your outputs feel lighter, but they land harder. Your network deepens. Your audience trusts faster. Your team anticipates without being told. The infrastructure you've built begins to absorb shock, adapt quickly, and accelerate progress, all while demanding less of your immediate energy.

This is the payoff for years of designing with intentionality. For building not just products or services, but systems, culture, and context. It's what happens when you've moved through the feedback loops enough times to understand what matters, and what never did. It's when your decision-making becomes faster, not because you're rushing, but because you're *pattern literate*.

The early years of obsession are hard. They're filled with ambiguity, false starts, overbuilding, underthinking, and lonely reinforcement. Most of what you're doing is invisible. Most of what you're learning feels slow. But in the background, something is taking shape, a body of work, a reputation, a clarity of voice, a network of believers. All of these are invisible until they aren't. And then they become your moat.

The Obsession Dividend shows up differently depending on what you've built. For creators, it might look like finally hitting escape velocity: your content spreads faster, your products sell longer, your offers convert without needing to push. For entrepreneurs, it might mean smoother fundraising, stronger teams, better hires, or customers who stay longer and spend more. For operators and builders within organizations, this might mean having influence, with your recommendations carrying weight, your fingerprints on core systems, and your leadership trusted across multiple layers.

But the most profound dividend isn't material. It's **internal**. You trust yourself. You've learned your cycles. You know what you're capable of. You know how to recover. How to re-enter. How to reset. You are not guessing. You are not hustling to prove something. You are building because it is your mode. Because you've shaped your identity around strategic purpose.

That internal dividend changes how you respond to volatility. You stop being reactive. You don't spiral into criticism. You don't chase every market shift. Because you've *built for something more profound than relevance*. You've built for resonance—and resonance compounds.

This phase is also when people start projecting their luck onto you. They'll assume things came easily, that the timing was perfect. You had help, but they didn't. But you know the truth: you earned the inflection point not in a single breakthrough, but in thousands of unseen iterations. In the years when no one clapped. In the days when you shipped even when it felt unclear. In the nights when you asked more complex questions, instead of lowering the standard.

The Obsession Dividend rewards those who stayed *true*, not trendy. Those who built leverage slowly, with taste and restraint. Those who could have taken shortcuts but didn't. It is a dividend not just on time invested, but on integrity maintained.

And it opens new possibilities. Because with leverage, you get to choose. You can go broader without losing depth. You can scale without breaking culture. You can start new experiments while the core machine hums quietly in the background. You're not chasing opportunity anymore, you're *curating* it.

But this is also when a new kind of threat emerges: complacency. When the system starts to work, the temptation is to coast. To stop questioning. To become defensive instead of curious. That's the trap. Because the dividend only continues if you remain obsessed. If you keep listening, sharpening, and protecting the clarity that got you here in the first place.

The dividend isn't a license to relax. It's an invitation to refine. To elevate. To bring even more intentionality to what you're building. Now that the foundation is solid, what can you do that you couldn't before? Who can you bring in? What parts of the mission can you accelerate, now that the machine can absorb the risk?

This phase is when the *legacy work* begins. You're no longer just surviving or proving. You're sculpting. Codifying. Teaching. Leaving behind more than just products or numbers, but systems, beliefs, and people who can carry the work forward.

This is also the point where obsession becomes **quiet**. Less fire. More architecture. Less noise. More signal. You're not chasing momentum anymore. You're controlling it. You're not trying to be known. You're working on what's worth knowing.

The Obsession Dividend isn't promised. It must be earned. But when it arrives, it changes everything. You are no longer trying to catch up on the work. The work is moving with you. You are no longer trying to convince the world. The world already knows.

Now, your job is to *steward* what you've built. To remain clear. To remain curious. And above all, to stay *obsessed*, not with outcomes, but with creating something that still matters a decade from now.

That is the absolute dividend: the ability to keep going, not because you have to, but because you *still want to*.

Chapter 40: The Final Layer

Every system has a surface. Then it has structure. Then it has code, logic, and protocol. But beneath it all, beneath the processes, strategies, and frameworks, is a final layer. Invisible, decisive, and definitive. In the life of the strategically obsessed, that final layer is **identity**.

This is where the obsession either sustains or collapses. Because no amount of systemization, planning, or output can outpace the limits of the person operating it, at some point, every builder must face the more profound truth: *you are building yourself while you build the work.*

The final layer isn't about tactics. It's about who you are becoming. Strategic obsession at scale cannot exist outside a well-forged identity. If the work grows and you don't, the gap becomes unbearable. The tension eats you alive. Either the mission shrinks to fit your comfort zone, or you fracture trying to carry what you haven't evolved to handle.

To finish the long game, you have to *become* the person who can finish it.

This doesn't happen accidentally. It happens through deliberate confrontation. You begin to study yourself, not just your strengths, but your defaults. Your reactive patterns. Your blind spots. You notice when control is masking fear, when overwork is masking inadequacy, when silence is masking misalignment.

The final layer of obsession demands that you be honest about what drives you. Because obsession has many masks: excellence, legacy, innovation, and leadership, but beneath each is a motive. Some pure. Some painful. The strategic obsessive doesn't run from this. They go toward it. They untangle it. They ask, "What part of this drive is mine, and what part is inherited performance?"

This is where the absolute freedom begins, not in doing more, but in *doing from clarity when* the work is no longer about validation, but expression, when the mission becomes an extension of your alignment, rather than a compensation for disconnection.

At this layer, obsession evolves. It softens, even as it sharpens. The need to prove disappears. The need to *build from truth* takes its place. You stop performing for the market and start speaking to the people who matter. You stop grasping for reach and start curating for resonance.

And your system changes. You no longer say yes to every invitation. You protect space not just for work, but for stillness. You build deeper relationships, not wider exposure. You start caring less about scale and more about substance.

This is what maturity inside obsession looks like: fewer swings, cleaner hits. Less speed, more precision. Less movement, more motion. You become selective not because you're tired, but because your signal is so clear that anything misaligned feels physically wrong.

But here's the most challenging part: the final layer often requires letting go of old versions of yourself. The one who hustled to be seen. The one who tolerated dilution for safety. The one who hid behind systems instead of building capacity. You must release what was helpful in one season to make what's necessary for the next.

This is why most people never reach the final layer. It requires ego death. Not self-doubt, but self-replacement. You have to become the kind of person who is no longer addicted to short-term reassurance. You have to train your nervous system to sit with ambiguity, to trust the architecture of the system when the emotions waver.

You start noticing your inner architecture just as much as your outer one. You care as much about your inputs, your reading, your conversations, and your solitude as you do about your outputs. You surround yourself with people who sharpen you, not flatter you. You seek mirrors, not megaphones.

At this point, obsession has become not a phase, or a strategy, or even a system, but an identity layer. Not one that traps you in a performance, but one that clarifies how you move through the world. You don't toggle in and out of obsession. You *are* obsessed with clarity, with alignment, with compounding good work that lasts.

And the result is that your work becomes *inevitable*. Not because it's loud, but because it's true. Not because it's hyped, but because it's earned. The final layer ensures that what you build outlasts the algorithm, the trend cycle, and he praise. It holds shape even if no one's watching, because it was never built *for* the watching.

This is the endgame of strategic obsession. Not hustle. Not an empire. But *the integrity of the system and the self*. A life where the work is not something you do to win approval, but the clearest expression of who you've become.

When you reach this layer, you don't stop. But you also don't strain. You move, cleanly, deliberately, with a kind of quiet intensity that requires no explanation. You are no longer trying to be something. You *are* it. And the system follows.

The final layer is not the end. It is the beginning of a life lived in alignment. A career built with clarity. A mission pursued with peace. That's what obsession gives you, not just momentum but *meaning*. Not just systems, but *selfhood*.

This is the dividend. This is the rhythm. This is the cost, and the reward. And when you build with this layer in place, everything compounds.

Not eventually. Now.

Epilogue

Becoming the System

In the beginning, there was you and an idea. Maybe fragile, maybe loud. Perhaps it came in a flash, or maybe it haunted you for years. You didn't know what it would become. You just knew you couldn't let it go. That idea became a path. That path required choices. And somewhere along the way, the ordinary ambition of "trying hard" gave way to something else entirely. **Obsession.**

Not the kind celebrated by hustle culture. Not the burnout theatre. Not the performative grind. But the quiet, strategic kind. The type that reshapes your days and rewrites your standards. The kind that doesn't ask for attention, it builds until it earns it. The kind that wakes you at 5 a.m., not because you have to, but because the work *pulls you.*

This book was never about productivity. It was never about hacks, or frameworks, or motivation. It was about building a life that can carry your biggest ideas, without breaking. About designing for alignment instead of applause. About creating systems so clean, so honest, so durable, that they carry you through every drift, dip, and reinvention.

That system doesn't start in software. It begins in **belief**. That something is worth compounding. That obsession, when designed well, is not a flaw but a force. That strategic obsession is the antidote to a distracted world.

173

The world will never stop offering you new priorities. It will always sell you noise, speed, and convenience. It will reward you for abandoning your path in favour of something more palatable, more viral, more profitable. It will ask you to trade your mission for relevance. Every day, that trade will be on the table.

This is where obsession becomes a *shield*. It protects you from the temptation of dilution. From the death by distraction. From the exhausting carousel of comparison. You don't need to be everywhere. You don't need to do everything. You need to keep building the *one thing that matters*.

And here's the secret: the more you protect that thing, the more power it gains. The longer you build in the same direction, the sharper your work becomes. The more repetitions, the more leverage. The more leverage, the more freedom. And the more freedom, the more dangerous you become, not to others, but to mediocrity.

There is no substitute for time served inside your system. There is no shortcut to taste, to timing, to clarity. That's what the obsessed understand: the goal is not just to finish something. The goal is to become *someone capable of finishing anything*.

And so, the work evolves. The identity evolves. The system evolves. You learn to move with rhythm instead of panic. You learn to lead with standards instead of noise. You stop broadcasting and start building. You stop reacting and start architecting.

Eventually, the lines blur. The system is no longer something you use. It is something you *are*.

You've become the infrastructure. The backbone. The consistency. The culture. People look at what you've built and wonder how you did it. And the answer is never magic. It's not luck. It's not access. It's that you kept going when it stopped being fun. You kept going when the dopamine ran out. You kept going when no one cared, and then *you earned the moment when they did.*

That's the dividend. That's the rhythm. That's the leadership. That's the final layer.

But don't stop here.

This isn't the kind of book you close and forget. This is the kind of book you come back to. In the dip. In the drift. In the inflection. Not because it has the answers, but because it reminds you that you already *chose.*

You chose to go deep. You decided to build with clarity. You chose obsession, not for attention, but for *alignment.*

So now the only question is:

Will you protect it?

Not once. Not sometimes. But always.

Because obsession isn't a phase.

It's the way through.

About The Author

David Webb is a seasoned entrepreneur and business leader with more than three decades of experience at the intersection of technology, finance, and services. As the founder and CEO of multiple ventures—some celebrated successes and some hard-learned failures—he has cultivated a reputation for turning complexity into clarity, driving growth, and leading organizations through periods of both turbulence and transformation. His career has been defined by a willingness to take calculated risks, embrace innovation, and pursue opportunities others often overlook.

David's debut book, Life Unscripted: What You Should Have Learned in High School, distilled years of professional and personal experience into a practical guide for navigating the overlooked realities of adulthood. His second work, The Book On Risk Management in Payments, marked a decisive step into specialized territory, tackling one of the most pressing challenges in global commerce: how to anticipate threats, safeguard trust, and manage risk in a world where money moves faster than regulation.

With his third book, The Book On Strategic Obsession: How to Turn Long-Term Thinking Into a Competitive Weapon, David advances his mission even further. Here he explores the discipline of sustained, long-horizon thinking as a defining advantage in leadership and strategy. Drawing from decades at the intersection of leadership, risk, and relentless execution, he challenges readers to rethink strategy—not as a plan on paper, but as an enduring obsession that separates fleeting achievements from lasting success.

Beyond writing and business, David remains committed to mentoring entrepreneurs and contributing to community initiatives that promote education, resilience, and personal growth. Whether in boardrooms, classrooms, or in print, his work reflects a consistent theme: empowering others to think critically, act decisively, and build systems that endure.

About The Publisher

Welcome to The Book On Publishing

At The Book On Publishing, we believe in rewriting the rules of learning. Whether you're chasing your next big idea, building a better life, or simply curious about what should have been taught in school, you've come to the right place.

We're a platform built for dreamers, doers, and lifelong learners—offering bold, practical books and tools that empower you to take charge of your journey. From real-world skills to mindset mastery, we publish the book on what matters.

No fluff. No lectures. Just what you need to know, delivered with clarity, purpose, and a spark of curiosity.

Start exploring. Start growing. Start writing your story.

Read more at https://thebookon.ca.

Acknowledgment of AI Assistance

Portions of this book were developed with the support of AI. While every word has been carefully reviewed and refined by the author, AI served as a valuable tool for brainstorming, editing, and structuring ideas. Its assistance helped accelerate the creative process and bring clarity to complex topics.